TENNIS
The Mind Game

Also by Marlin M. Mackenzie

GOLF: THE MIND GAME
SKIING: THE MIND GAME

TENNIS

The Mind Game

Marlin M. Mackenzie, Ed.D.,
with Ken Denlinger

A DELL TRADE PAPERBACK

A DELL TRADE PAPERBACK
Published by
Dell Publishing
a division of
Bantam Doubleday Dell
Publishing Group, Inc.
1540 Broadway
New York, New York 10036

Designed by Richard Oriolo

The trademark Dell® is registered in the U.S.
Patent and Trademark Office.

ISBN: 0-440-50271-3

Printed in the United States of America

Published simultaneously in Canada

April 1991

10 9 8 7 6 5 4 3 2

BVG

CONTENTS

vi   Contents

x

ACKNOWLEDGMENTS

Lots of people shared directly and indirectly in the development of this book and the one before it, *Golf: The Mind Game.* They were athletes from many different sports, my students, my collaborating author, my agent, my editor, and most of all my wife, Edna.

A dozen or so outstanding tennis players were exceedingly helpful because they allowed me to rummage around in their brains to find out how their minds work. And they provided the true test of the validity of my techniques when they actually performed better after using them.

My graduate students at Teachers College, Columbia University, constantly challenged me as I trained them to become sports counselors. Their analytical minds and healthy skepticism enabled me to refine and expand my techniques.

My collaborator, Ken Denlinger, was a constant source of humor, understanding, encouragement, practicality, and skepticism.

My agent, Faith Hornby Hamlin, had the insight and confidence to recognize that my earliest draft of a book for athletes in general contained the seeds of a publishable book; and she obviously persuaded others to agree with her.

My editor, Jody Rein, with the force of her logical analysis and organization, and with her interest in my approach, guided my collaborator and me in transforming our original manuscript into a series of books on the mind game in several sports.

Edna, my wife and companion, deserves a hearty hug and

immeasurable thanks for her emotional support and for her hours of careful editing of draft after draft after draft of my manuscript. She demanded clarity, logic, and good grammar without imposing upon me her own ideas about competition and play or about mental processes.

To all of these people I say, "Thanks!" To the tennis players among them I say, "Have a good time and play well."

MMM
Washingtonville, New York

People pay dearly to play tennis. Top to bottom, they spend as much as $500 to at least look formidable to that opponent across the net. And the racquet, which still resembles something used by early Americans to swat grime from the living room carpet, might run to $160. At those prices tennis becomes quite an investment. Yet nearly all players, from humble hackers to elite touring pros, in dogged pursuit of enjoyment—and victory—rarely invest as much as a thought in what will help them more than any hunk of high-tech equipment: their own minds.

I propose to change that. In this book I explain the ways your mind, more marvelous than any computer, can be tapped to improve your tennis game. Wouldn't you like to feel the ball jump more consistently from the sweet spot of your racquet, producing more winners and necessitating fewer tiebreakers?

What I offer is a practical, down-to-earth system that uses the mind and emotions to regulate tennis shots that fulfill your game plans—and this system *works*, whether you're a weekend enthusiast or a world-class professional, a club player with a pretty good second serve who can sustain fairly long rallies at the baseline or a computer-ranked player who can hold his own in professional tournaments. The system works because it quiets the conscious mind and engages your unconscious resources. An active, conscious mind acts like the net—it blocks you from playing your best because you're *thinking* too much about your stroke mechanics while playing. My techniques get you to do all your thinking about your swing and game plan during practice sessions so that your conscious mind stays out of the way during a match.

After years of coaching and thinking about the unity of mind and body, I became dissatisfied with the methods of coaching that stressed conscious thought. The methods are okay up to a point, but they don't fully represent what superb athletes really do in their minds to control their behavior.

To eliminate my dissatisfaction I studied psychology and counseling; finally I decided to go to the source. I asked athletes directly how they used their minds and emotions to develop and control their skills. My training as a Master Practitioner in Neuro-Linguistic Programming (NLP) provided me with the knowledge to ask the right questions and the skills to uncover the athletes' conscious and unconscious mental processes.

I then created counseling techniques out of what the athletes told me. I combined their information with what I'd learned from psychology and from my coaching experience. I coined a word that describes my perspective of how the mind works in sports—*metaskills*. It refers to the interaction between emotions and thoughts that produce skillful athletic performance, most of which are outside conscious awareness.

To refine my metaskills techniques I worked directly with 80 elite athletes (male and female, ages eight to thirty-five) in 11 sports over two years. The model that evolved has been working successfully for about seven years with all kinds of athletes. This book contains those techniques that are most appropriate for tennis players.

Although tennis can be a complex mind game, it's also supposed to be fun. Yet the faces of amateur and professional players on the court suggest either war or depression instead of enjoyment. So the exercises in this book are designed to be fun, to lighten up the tennis game so you can both play better and enjoy it more. I describe in Part I the fundamentals of the mind game: how your mind operates, how to deepen awareness of your mental processes, and how to improve your game by capitalizing on your inner resources.

Part II contains descriptions of specific techniques, about 30 in all, that can be applied to your method of thinking and the unique way you respond emotionally to competition. These techniques are designed to help you achieve better concentration, heightened motivation, consistency of performance, increased self-confidence, recovery of lost skills, and more enjoyment. A few of them focus on the mobilization of energy when you're tired, faster healing after injury, and pain control.

The psychological perspective that I emphasize is one of understanding *How* tennis players, at every level, control their performance, not *Why* they don't play well. Believe it or not, you already possess all the necessary internal resources for playing better tennis. The trick is to uncover them and put them to work. Trying to figure out the reasons why you don't hit the ball well is counterproductive. This kind of thinking taps and reinforces negative stuff in your mind, the stuff that makes you continue to hit the ball badly and feel worse.

The mind games in this book are designed to swing your tennis mind from conscious control to automatic pilot. The ultimate goal is to have your unconscious mind in complete control during competition, except for occasional review of your overall game plan. Seldom will you need to consciously apply any metaskills techniques while playing a match. If you've learned them well, they'll "kick in" automatically, just as your best tennis stroke automatically follows a grooved pattern.

What Will This Book Do for you?

The metaskills techniques will improve your tennis game by changing the way you think and feel. You'll learn how your mind regulates your tennis shots. You'll learn how to expand and modify your sensory apparatus so your thinking is changed. You'll learn how your emotions can be controlled so your mind can work smoothly and unconsciously. You'll learn how to use self-hypnosis to identify your mental resources. In short, you'll learn to have more choices about how to hit a tennis ball so that your game improves and your sense of enjoyment is enhanced.

If you're a club player, metaskills techniques won't get you an invitation to Wimbledon. Still, they'll get you a stronger second serve, if that's a goal, or get you to hit crisper and deeper shots consistently from the baseline. Using them will make you as fine at specific skills as your ability permits and better able to cope with such miseries as receiving a booming service when it's 6–5 in the tiebreaker of the final set.

This book will help you get into the just-right state so your mental tennis-shot programs will take over. You'll learn to get your conscious mind out of the way, stop talking to yourself, stop doing anything, and just let go when you swing your racquet.

How to Use This Book

Use this book to supplement the work of your tennis pro, whose job it is to teach you the actual mechanics of tennis. You can read it whenever you have a spare moment and refer to it during your practice sessions.

The time frame for learning any one of the techniques can range from half an hour to a few weeks. It all depends on what you want and how much energy you give to getting it. Mental practice, like physical practice, also requires time.

I can't emphasize often enough that the best way to learn my techniques is to experience them firsthand, while *doing* something—volleying, for instance, or serving kick serves—something very precise that you would like to improve. First, find out what happens to the way you play tennis; analyze and evaluate the usefulness of a technique in terms of your improvement, not in terms of whether my approach fits existing psychological theory.

The goal is to have your unconscious mind in complete control during competition. Seldom will there be a need for conscious application of any metaskills techniques while playing a match. If you've learned them well, they'll take over automatically, just as your ideal tennis stroke follows a grooved pattern.

Controlling your tennis shots comes from the inside out, first consciously, then unconsciously. Your beliefs and values, your emotions and your thought processes regulate the quality of your game and the extent of your enjoyment. My metaskills techniques are based on tapping your unconscious resources through your senses and getting your conscious mind out of your way.

While this is not a workbook, it nonetheless should be a learning companion when you're practicing the skills taught to you by your tennis pro. For a while, don't leave home for the courts without it. Treat it as a learning manual to help you use your mind and emotions to get what you want. Read Part I carefully and do the exercises presented there. This will make the rest of the book more meaningful. After doing the Sherlock Holmes Exercise and learning how to "anchor" your internal resources, read Part II casually. Then study and use the appropriate techniques in Part II when something in your game or some aspect of temperament needs to be retuned or cleared up.

Not every lesson is for you. The final chapter, "Game, Set, Match," tells you how to identify your desired outcomes and guides you in selecting appropriate metaskills techniques to achieve them. However, I encourage you to pay attention to only the crucial elements of your game you want to improve. I'm a firm believer in the notion "If it ain't broke, don't fix it."

Setting aside mental-practice time is essential to learning my metaskills techniques. Merely *reading* this book is not enough. And *do only one exercise at a time.* Learn how it works and determine whether it fits your mental style. Some of my best clients initially experienced "brain lock" when they tried to use too many of my exercises at once. They learned, the hard way, the importance of exploring one technique at a time.

Which mind games will be most useful for you? Only you can determine that. Happy exploring.

I

The Fundamentals

Learning how the mind works, how to make it work more efficiently, and how to tap your internal resources are the first steps to master in the tennis player's mind game. The initial part of this book is as fundamental as learning how to keep score or grip the racquet. Not until the fundamentals are learned will you be able to swing your mind so that you accomplish what may seem self-contradictory: swinging the racquet with effortless effort and mindless concentration.

Settle back into an easy chair now and put aside your point of view about hitting a tennis ball. In this first part of the book I'll present some basic ideas about the mind and how to run your brain. Then I'll have you become your own investigator to explore how your mind actually plays your game. After explaining how the pros use their minds while playing, I'll provide you with special exercises to expand your mental capacities. Finally you'll learn a special way to uncover and use your internal resources.

ONE

The Warm-Up

As a 15-year-old, Michael Gratz was a highly skilled tennis player with a problem as common—and frustrating—as a cold. He could serve and rush the net well enough to put his opponent on the defensive. But when a lob was thrown up to his backhand side, he clutched and either missed the ball completely or sprayed shots into nearby courts, into the net, and over the fence—everywhere except where he wanted them to go.

A few years ago Michael uttered two words familiar to me and to everyone else for whom skilled performance is a mystery: "What's wrong?"

I believe answering a question like that isn't very useful. I focused on the solution—what Michael can do *right*—instead of what he may be doing wrong.

I asked him, "Have you ever in your life seen anyone hit backhand overheads the way you want to hit them?" Of course he had. He had watched Billie Jean King hit a brilliant winner in Madison Square Garden just the week before.

I told him to re-create in his mind that beautifully played

shot of Billie Jean's in as much detail as possible. How did the swing look? Could he recall the sound of the racquet's impact on the ball as she put it away? Could he feel the shot as he watched it again? I put him through a series of exercises on the court that were designed to train his mind to mimic Billie Jean's shot. Later he was able to execute it unconsciously.

Michael had an inkling of how to learn that shot all along because he had copied other tennis strokes of greats like Bjorn Borg and Jimmy Connors. I helped him realize that and how he could capitalize on his own resources for learning. I find that all of us have resources tucked away in various parts of our minds. They can be retrieved rather quickly, with a unique search process, and then applied with a key to make them stick. Michael uncovered his mental resource of mimicry and created his own key to make his overheads splendid put-aways.

Michael's key was a metaphor, the thought of flicking a fly into a basket. It was a metaphor that integrated his thoughts and body and allowed his unconscious mind to swing the racquet so that the ball would consistently land in an open court.

How Michael learned the shot and created his metaphor will be explained fully in a subsequent chapter. For now it's only important to realize that all the mind games in this book reflect Michael's experience. They are unusual and fun, and they work. They are based on a couple of very simple and basic ideas: the unity of mind and body and the power of the unconscious mind.

Mind-Body Unity

The fundamental principle underlying my perspective of human behavior in general, and athletic performance in particular, is that mind, body, and emotions are inextricably interwoven. It's sort of like having your two hands pressed together as one on a two-hand backhand shot.

Thought influences feelings and performance; feelings affect thought and performance; and performance affects thought and feelings. Specifically the quality and consistency of your athletic performance depend on *how* you think and *how* you feel emotionally.

The metaskills techniques presented in this book were designed to affect your thought processes and emotional states, with only minimal attention to the content of your thoughts.

The Unconscious Mind in Sports

Think about thinking. Thinking while executing sports skills is detrimental because it destroys intense concentration. In Zen meditation the ideal state of concentration is paying attention to nothing. This applies to swinging a tennis racquet as well, but it is extremely difficult to achieve. The next best way of thinking is to pay attention to *only one thing*. It might be watching the ball, feeling your grip, hearing a phrase spoken in your head, or seeing an image in your mind's eye—whatever works for you.

For instance, if Mary Lou Retton had had to process mentally every bit of information necessary to execute that perfect 10 vault in the 1984 Olympics—feet together at takeoff, hands exactly so to get into the twist, knees bent at a precise moment while in the air—she never would have landed on a Wheaties box.

Instead Mary Lou tied every bit of complex movement into a single word. That word was *stick*. She knew unconsciously what was necessary to achieve perfection, to "stick" a 10 and to "stick" to the mat after a flawless trip. She used that word to trigger her unconscious mind, which automatically guided her body to achieve Olympian power and grace.

I know the paramount role the unconscious mind has in affecting human behavior. Superb athletic performance is achieved with little or no *conscious* thought given to goals, tactics, and mechanics. The clichés that reinforce this are numerous: "paralysis by analysis," "playing in the zone," and "It's like I wasn't there."

Conscious processing is entirely too slow and results in confusion. You don't think about hitting a baseball; you just do it. If you thought about how to connect with a slider, low and outside, the umpire would have his thumb jerked in the air for strike three before the bat got off your shoulder.

The more refined the athlete's performance, the more the unconscious mind is in control. While conscious attention to performance is most important during learning and practice, it is the mindless (unconscious) processes that allow for exquisite execution of skills already mastered.

Neuro-Linguistic Programming

During the past 15 years a new psychotechnology has emerged. It's called Neuro-Linguistic Programming (NLP); it was created by Richard Bandler and John Grinder. Essentially a multipurpose technology of communication, it is used to identify how people actually regulate their behavior with their minds. It is used to help people change their behavior rather quickly by changing mental processes. NLP is a vital part of my work because it emphasizes the role of the unconscious mind in regulating behavior.

In my opinion NLP is one of the most powerful psychological tools available to help people change their behavior. It is state-of-the-art theory and practice based on verbal and nonverbal communication processes. Increasing numbers of psychologists and psychiatrists are coming to recognize its usefulness in overcoming phobias, compulsions, stage fright, and other debilitating behaviors. If you're interested in learning more about NLP, you'll find selected readings listed in the back of the book. They will give you an in-depth understanding of this new approach to changing human behavior.

The elements of the NLP model that apply to tennis are *information processing, mental strategies, emotional states,* and *beliefs and values.*

Information Processing and Mental Strategies

Let's look a little closer at the way your tennis-playing mind works. How does someone know how to swing a racquet? For that matter, how does anyone know how to drive a car or do anything else? By reproducing in his mind the sights, sounds, feelings, smells, and tastes associated with how he did it in the past.

In a span of two or three seconds, the time it takes to swing a racquet, we unconsciously process as many as a hundred bits of patterned, or programmed, sensory information—sights, sounds, and feelings—to control our behavior. This programmed information, or strategy, fires off just nanoseconds in advance of a behavior such as hitting a blazing down-the-line topspin winner. If the tennis player's swing program is wrong or is interrupted, he has an unforced error.

The mental programming we've developed for ourselves over a lifetime is much more sophisticated than anything that could be put on a floppy disk. And the nice thing about our programs is that they're flexible. We can change them at a moment's notice when we sense, consciously or unconsciously, that they ought to be altered for our own best interests.

We often find several separate strategies in operation to regulate a number of different behaviors at the same time. For example, consider a right-handed player at the net whose return is lobbed deep to his left. First he must initiate his decision-making strategy to determine whether the ball will land in the court and whether he should attempt to retrieve it. If he decides to go after it, his motivation strategy is energized to carry out that decision.

Since the lob is not exactly like any previous lob, he sets his creativity strategy in motion to put together a new combination of movements to get him back to the ball and in position to hit it well. Knowing exactly how to return the lob to an open court also requires that his memory strategy be set off. Then, to execute the shot he has in mind, he activates his performance strategy.

Whew!

Within several seconds, or much less time than it took you to read this, he triggered five separate strategies: *decision making, motivation, creativity, memory,* and *performance.* Each strategy was somewhat dependent on the others. Unconscious thought, that which is outside awareness, was much more significant to his athletic performance than conscious thought. And the more streamlined the mental process, the faster his reaction—or that of any athlete.

This complex form of mentally regulating human behavior is called a *cybernetic system.* Feedforward and feedback mechanisms are constantly in operation as the athlete performs, usually outside conscious awareness. The internal regulatory systems of the body are constantly comparing

ongoing internal and external sensory data with the output of
the muscles that bring about our intended behavior, like
hitting a tennis ball.

Let's say you're a serve-and-volleyer rushing the net
behind your serve. To plan for your next shot you need both
present and past information to feed forward into the plan.
That information consists of your opponent's tendency to
return the kind of ball you served, the motion of his body and
racquet as he swings at your serve, and the speed and
trajectory of his return. This information, all processed
unconsciously, regulates how fast you should move and in
what direction to hit your opponent's shot.

As you move toward the spot from which you expect to
make your return, other information is being fed back to your
unconscious mind to help you adjust your movements. That
information includes the speed of your movement in relation
to the ball, your balance, how the racquet feels in your hand,
the alignment of your body as you set up for the shot, the
wind blowing across the court, and the position of your
opponent.

Comparisons of information are continuously and rapidly
being made in your brain, automatically and unconsciously,
between information that is fed forward and information that
is fed back. If the feedback information doesn't match the
feedforward information, information must continue to be
gathered to help you change the way you hit the ball. When
the comparisons between feedforward and feedback information match, no change in the planned return shot is initiated.
Voilà! You execute a smoothly executed, crosscourt slice
that lands on the sideline in front of the service line for a
winner. Your unconscious mind is so sensitive that it even
reacts and adjusts to an unexpected breeze.

Metaskills techniques are designed to affect the basic
elements of the tennis player's unconscious mental strate-

gies. They are based on how the brain actually works when the conscious mind doesn't interfere with it. The techniques are designed to change or stabilize a player's performance by changing how, in his mind, he processes sights, sounds, feelings, smells, and tastes.

Just-Right Emotional State

Although people's programmed mental strategies for hitting tennis balls are different, what's common to all of us is the fact that we must be in an appropriate mood or emotional state for a particular strategy to be activated. And each of us has unique just-right states for accomplishing different tasks. When you are in the just-right state for, say, a kick serve, the patterned sequence of all of the auditory, visual, and kinesthetic information that represents your experience of having done that task before is automatically and unconsciously fired off before and during the execution of the stroke. However, if you're not in the right state, the strategy for the task will be defective because key elements in it are missing.

I'm sure you know that the state you want to be in while going for a down-the-line forehand topspin winner will be much different from the state you want to be in when you slice a dink shot. For the former you want to muster the power and control to hug the line; for the latter you want a delicate touch to just clear the net.

Because your emotional state determines whether you will play well or not, many of my metaskills techniques are based on identifying and anchoring the appropriate internal states for hitting different tennis shots. When they're properly anchored, the appropriate strategy will be engaged and the shot will be executed automatically. Getting into those just-right states is part of what this book is about.

Beliefs and Values

Tennis players can't leave their beliefs and values behind when they head out to the court. A belief is something accepted as true without certainty of proof; a value is a standard or criterion by which you determine if something is important to you. Both serve as guides to making decisions, and both are at work during every tennis match, affecting the player's moods from moment to moment. Since moods influence mental strategies, beliefs and values either facilitate or intrude on what could be a very pleasurable tennis match.

Compare the emotional responses of two different players in a best-of-three-sets match when the player is down one set and 2–4 in the second. One player values winning and perfection and believes victory should be based on expert performance. If he had a lot of unforced errors, his emotional response will probably be dejection; he also thinks he doesn't deserve to win because he believes he has been playing poorly.

Another player, however, might respond positively to the same situation; his attitude could be that here is an unprecedented chance to learn what has prevented him from playing up to his potential. The first player is controlled by values pertaining to perfection and winning; the second, in exactly the same context, is influenced by his belief in the value of any experience as an opportunity to learn and change.

The first player is dejected, the second curious and optimistic. The chances that the second player will recover to win the second set and perhaps the match are certainly higher than for the first player because the second player's emotional state, influenced by his beliefs and values, is more conducive to good play.

In many instances changing and reordering your values and beliefs can affect your performance—this book will help you to do just that.

Communication and Change

The techniques in this book are forms of communication that are intended to change your behavior. They are designed to influence your mental strategies, your emotional states, and your beliefs and values. My instructions are deliberately intended to affect the *way* you perceive the environment and the *way* you communicate with yourself—the *way* you run your brain. Your attention will be limited to how you process relevant sights, sounds, and feelings, *not* focused on how to prepare, swing, and hit the ball. My techniques do not teach you the physical mechanics of getting into the proper position, of gripping the racquet and swinging it; that's the tennis pro's job. However, while you are learning the mechanics of tennis, or after you have learned them, my mental techniques will help you execute them better.

Self-Hypnosis

Some of my exercises are based on hypnosis, although highly sophisticated daydreaming might be as good a way to describe some of what actually happens. It's Walter Mitty stuff, nothing scary. Most athletes, in fact, are in a trance, a profound altered state, when they perform superbly.

Admit it, now. You've transported yourself, perhaps at a traffic light or at the office, to the finals at the U.S. Open, needing to win only one more game at sold-out Flushing Meadows for unimagined glory, not to mention a fistful of dollars. In your mind you see an array of your best serves, passing shots, overheads, and net volleys that might accomplish that.

Growing up, you watched Sandy Koufax, Arnold Palmer, Billie Jean King, and other wondrous athletes. Later you tried to mimic their seemingly unique motions in your mind—and then scooted outside and worked on duplicating them. What surely never entered your mind at the time is that you were using a kind of self-hypnosis. I have techniques that use that concept, one of which helped young Michael learn to hit overheads like Billie Jean King. This technique, which I'll explain in full later, took just a few minutes, and Michael was in an altered state much of the time. Although he was hitting tennis balls, his mind was on flicking a fly into a basket.

Let's get started.

The Sherlock Holmes Exercise: Discover How Your Mind Regulates Your Tennis Shots

This is a must-read chapter; it's fundamental to everything that follows. Practically all of my techniques deal with "going inside" and retrieving past experiences. These remembered experiences are resources to be used to refine your game and make it more consistent. And being able to identify these resources on command is essential to playing my unique mind games. How to go about doing that is what you'll learn in this chapter.

Be Sherlock Holmes for a while and discover the important elements of your game. All you have to think about is being wonderful, in your own mind, at least. As Sherlock you'll be searching for clues to what makes your performance so special. These clues will be in the form of sights, sounds, and feelings, some of which will eventually become important cues to running your brain effectively while on the court.

It's important that you go to a quiet place to do this exercise. When you do, you will recall when you made a particularly fine shot and relive it in exquisite detail. You'll think about a very specific shot, not an entire match or game or even a whole point. Out of the hundreds or thousands of shots you've hit, simply select one that made you proud. Maybe it was a down-the-line forehand that hugged the line, or a crosscourt backhand winner, or a service ace that finished off a match.

The idea of this exercise is to uncover some of the crucial elements of the mental program that regulates your movements while preparing for and then hitting the ball; this is known as a strategy. That strategy contains a series of representations of sensory bits of information—sights, sounds, and feelings. I use the letters *V, A,* and *K* to signify those sensory bits; V is for visual, A is for auditory, and K is for kinesthetic—muscle and joint feelings, feelings on the surface of your body, and the bodily sensations associated with emotions.

During the execution of a tennis shot, starting with getting into the proper position, continuing with taking the racquet back, and ending with the follow-through after striking the ball, your mind processes as many as 100 bits of sensory information with machine-gun rapidity. Just a few of those sensory representations are in your conscious awareness. The rest are processed unconsciously because of the speed of the ball and the quickness of the stroke itself.

Sensory information consists of specific internal sights, sounds, and feelings representing specific *past* experiences of preparing for and hitting a tennis ball; it also consists of *ongoing* internal and external sights, sounds, and feelings that are occurring as you play a shot.

Your Task as
Sherlock Holmes

The way you watch your past performance, the way you listen to the sounds associated with it, and the kind of bodily sensations that you pay attention to will determine your success as Sherlock Holmes. The more thorough you are, the more clues that make your performance so good will be discovered.

The main questions to ask yourself as you relive that shot are these: What were the things you saw, the things you heard, and the things you felt that let you know where to position yourself on the court and when and how to swing the racquet? What did you see, hear, and feel that let you know that your movements were either okay or needed to be corrected?

You're looking for clues—in the form of certain A's, V's, and K's—that control what you already know how to do but may not know that you know. You might notice, for example, that you had a firm but light grip on the racquet; that K is a clue. Or you may hear the sound of the ball rebounding from your racquet strings; that A is a clue. Or you might notice the spin of the ball as it approaches you; that V is a clue. Make mental notes of the A's, V's, and K's as you go along. At the end of the search you can write down what you discovered.

Later you will learn which of these clues are of significance to the way you mentally regulate your tennis shots. Some of them will be of no consequence; others will be vital and will serve as visual, auditory, and kinesthetic cues to stimulate your unconscious mental processes. The metaskills exercises in Part II will help you know which sensory bits of information are the most useful.

Now let's begin.

Step 1. General Review

In your mind, go back to the time and place when you made that fine shot. First, just do a general, overall review of it, as if you're watching a sound movie. Forget about the specta-tors. Just pay attention to the sensory bits of information—

what you saw, heard, and felt—that regulated your shot. Those bits of information could be related to how you approached the ball, your preparation and body position, grip, swing, and the mood or state you were in.

See the court where you were playing and the trajectory, speed, and direction of the ball coming from your opponent. Of course, if it's your own serve that you're thinking about, then just notice whether you were serving to the deuce or ad court. Notice the light and shadows and the brightness of the colors. See the images that were in your mind as you were making that shot. Maybe you were imagining the flight of the ball or the swing path of your racquet.

Hear again what you heard then, both on the outside and inside your mind. Perhaps you heard the *whoosh* of your racquet and the "sound" of your own voice giving yourself silent instructions. Pay attention to the loudness and pitch and tempo of the sounds. As you see and hear those things, *feel* again what you felt during your preparation and swing— the coordinated movements of your body and the tension and relaxation of your muscles. Also, become aware of the mood or emotional state you were in as you were hitting the ball.

Now it's time to get out Holmes's magnifying glass and ear trumpet and pay more attention to the details of what you saw, heard, and felt back then, on the outside and inside your mind.

Step 2. Identifying the V's—the Sights

First pay attention to what you saw on the outside as if you were right there on the court, standing or moving toward the ball and making that shot. I call these images "regular" pictures. Then shift your way of watching so that you see yourself hitting the ball as if looking through someone else's eyes. It might be helpful to imagine stepping out of your body, walking a few paces, and then turning to gaze upon a piece of athletic magic about to unfold from your favorite athletic star—you.

From this visual perspective, called the *metaposition,* take the role of Sherlock Holmes and search for something that you didn't know you knew that made your shot so good.

As you watch yourself perform, change the image of yourself—the *metapicture*—to color if it's black and white; change it to black and white if it's in color. If the picture is bright, make it dull; if dull, make it bright. If the picture is sharply defined, make it fuzzy; if fuzzy, make it defined. Notice what happens to the quality of your performance as you vary the internal images this way; your performance may get better or worse. Does your swing get better or worse as you vary the color, brightness, focus, and size of the pictures? Make mental notes about the kinds of images that made your performance good.

Now make regular pictures of the shot, no longer watching yourself. See again what you saw while preparing for and making the shot. Vary the color, brightness, and definition of what you saw as you were swinging the racquet. Continue to search for the important clues that let you know when and how to swing. Look for the clues that let you know whether your movements were okay or needed to be changed. Notice what happens to the quality of your performance as you vary the images. Does it improve or deteriorate?

Now take a moment to become aware of the *internal* images, the ones you had in your mind *then,* when you were making the shot. What were they, if any? Did you see an image of the proper grip? Did you see an imaginary line directing you to the target? How were these internal images helpful? Vary the color, brightness, and definition of these internal images; notice what happens to the quality of your performance as you vary them. Does it get better or worse?

Step 3. Identifying the A's—The Sounds

While watching your past performance, using either regular pictures or metapictures, hear again what you heard then. Listen to the sounds directly associated with moving to the ball and swinging the racquet. Listen to the sounds in the surrounding environment and the sounds in your mind. For instance, on the outside you might hear your feet striking the ground as you moved to the ball or the ball striking the strings of your racquet. On the inside, in your mind, you might hear silence or your own voice giving yourself instructions.

If the sounds were loud, make them barely audible; if hardly heard, turn up the volume. If they were high-pitched tones, make them low; if low-pitched, make them high. If they were harmonious, make them discordant and unpleasant; if unpleasant, make them harmonious. If the tempo of the sounds was an even beat, make it irregular; if irregular, make it even. And while you're varying the sounds, notice whether the quality of your performance improves or deteriorates. Continue, as Sherlock Holmes, to listen for the important sounds that were present when your movements were just as they were supposed to be. Are some sounds more important than others? Make a mental note of your discoveries.

Step 4. Identifying the K's—The Bodily Sensations

As you relive the shot over and over, pay close attention to (1) the feelings of your coordinated movements, (2) the feelings of certain parts of your body that were essential to making the shot, (3) the amount of energy and tension you felt in various muscles, and (4) the emotional feelings or mood you were in *while* you were hitting the ball.

You might feel a number of things as you do this exercise. For instance, you might feel the turn of your shoulders on the backswing, or the strength of your grip on the racquet, or the shifting of your weight from one foot to another.

Now, in your mind, vary the way you moved. If your movements were quick, slow them down; if slow, speed them up. If you were exerting a lot of energy and pressure, relax the effort; if effortless, increase the tension of your muscles. While varying those feelings, notice what happens to the quality of your performance. Does it get better or worse? As Sherlock Holmes, continue to identify and make mental notes of the feelings that made your performance so good.

The emotional feelings you had in your body *while,* not after, you were approaching and hitting the ball are as important as the muscular feelings associated with making the shot. Those bodily emotional sensations represent the mood or state you were in. Feel them again. Perhaps they were feelings of lightness, tingling, warmth, tension, or pulsing that were present in parts of your body. Vary the intensity of these emotional feelings and find out what happens to the quality of the shot. Does it get better or worse when you increase or decrease the intensity? What amount of intensity is just right for making it the best possible shot?

Step 5. Putting It All Together

After you've gone through seeing, listening, and feeling, have some fun with reliving that past performance. Pretend you've got a videotape of it and watch it while using the variable-speed and direction buttons on the video control.

First run the tape twice as fast as normal, then four times as fast, and then bring the speed back to normal. In addition, slow the tape down to half speed and then to one frame at a time. Be sure to bring the tape back up to normal speed. With each variation in speed, carefully pay attention, as before, to discovering new visual, auditory, and kinesthetic clues to what seem to be essential to hitting the ball so well.

Now run the tape in reverse—in normal, slow, and fast

motion—again paying attention to new sights, sounds, and feelings. Finish up by running the tape forward again. Keep in mind that the usefulness of the sensory information you uncover will be determined as you work with the metaskills techniques described later on.

Here is a summary of the steps to follow.

SHERLOCK HOLMES EXERCISE

1. Go to a quiet room. With practice you'll be able to do it out on the court.

2. Remember a specific shot that you hit during a match.

3. See everything you can see about the shot; hear everything you can hear about the shot; feel everything you can feel about the shot.

4. Vary what you see (from color to black-and-white, from fuzzy to clear); change the sounds (from loud to soft, from pleasant to unpleasant); alter your feelings (from quick to slow, from relaxed to tense).

5. Remember the details. Write the important ones down if it'll help. You'll be using them later on.

Reactions to the
Sherlock Holmes Exercise

Although there are some typical sensory information that most tennis players pay attention to while they're making a shot, each person has his or her unique way of processing and giving meaning to particular A's, V's, and K's. There are no right or wrong sensory cues for playing tennis. It's what you do with them that's important.

To help you understand how professional tennis players process information, I'll share with you some of what I learned from them when they used the Sherlock Holmes Exercise. Their mental processes are often unusual and quite sophisticated. I'll identify both their *internal* and *external* sensory representations.

Internal sensations—what a person sees, hears, and feels inside, in the mind—are classified in NLP lingo as "downtime." External sensations—what a person sees, hears, and feels that come directly from the environment or are directly associated with movements that control their tennis shots—are classified in NLP lingo as "uptime."

What the Pros See—The Internal (Downtime) V's

All pros that I've talked to imagine the actual trajectory they want the ball to follow before hitting it. Their internal motion picture images include the location where they want the ball to bounce in their opponent's court.

JoAnne Russell, a former tennis professional, has a picture of herself making the shot at hand just before getting to the ball. For a second or two she mentally steps outside of her body, looking at herself as if she were in the gallery behind the court. This image guides her preparation and swing. Some professionals see themselves from the side rather than from behind the court.

Mike Estep is a former professional player who has coached Hana Mandlikova and Martina Navratilova. During his competitive days he usually made an internal image of how his opponent tended to move after hitting certain kinds of shots under certain circumstances; accordingly, he planned his upcoming shot to take advantage of his opponent's uncovered court. Another former professional player, Bruce Manson, did almost the same thing, except he became aware of spontaneous mental images of his opponent's usual shots; in this way he anticipated his opponent's next shot, giving him a jump start on his own return.

What the Pros See—The External (Uptime) V's

Uptime *visual* cues that pros attend to are familiar to you, I'm sure, because most tennis players are sensitive to them. They include the ball, court lines, the net, the court position of their opponent, the angle of the opponent's racquet head during each stroke, and their opponent's facial expression.

What the Pros Hear—The Internal (Downtime) A's

The internal auditory information processed by professional tennis players almost always consists of short, positive statements or commands. Diane Desfor, a former Women's Tennis Association (WTA) competitor, reminds herself, "Be ready!" when she's about to receive service. When she's playing her best, Terry Phelps, WTA player currently on tour, tells herself to "hit it hard" and sings silently to herself while hitting ground strokes; the song matches the rhythm of her stroke.

Many other pros, however, are aware of only internal silence when they are playing well. When playing poorly, they silently admonish themselves for their mistakes. One ranked senior player hears, in his mind, the loud, harsh, critical voice of his father when he makes an unforced error; when he's playing well, he repeatedly and emphatically says to himself, "Do it!" To keep herself alert and motivated, a young, successful amateur player says, "Let's go!"

Barbara Potter, former tour player, says that she "hears her body working" when she's playing well—a kind of resonant sound of being physically tuned up.

What the Pros Hear—The
External (Uptime) A's

The significant uptime *auditory* cues that pros listen to are the sound of the ball on their opponent's racquet, the sound of the ball's bounce on the court, their opponent's footsteps, the *whoosh* of the racquet during the stroke, and the sound of the ball striking their own racquet strings.

What the Pros Feel—The
Internal (Downtime) K's

The way tennis players feel emotionally on the inside is absolutely crucial to playing tennis consistently well. As you might expect, the emotional state most conducive for good play varies from person to person and from time to time.

Terry Phelps is aware of being relaxed, seeing a variety of pleasant scenes when she's playing her best. JoAnne Russell is acutely aware of lightness in her body when she is in top form. At times John McEnroe apparently needs to be in a state of anger if he is to play well.

The just-right state—the internal emotion K's—for playing various points and for hitting various shots are perhaps the most important internal clues to identify; and the ability to generate those states quickly is undoubtedly the most important mental skill you can learn. Chapters 4, 5, and 6 are devoted to this important process.

What the Pros Feel—The
External (Uptime) K's

The most important uptime *kinesthetic* cues of the pros are associated with the grip and stroke mechanics. JoAnne

Russell hardly feels her grip on the racquet, it's so light. Peter Burwash, one of today's outstanding tennis coaches, encourages his students to feel the acceleration of the wrist action at the point of contact with the ball. And John McEnroe is exquisitely aware of his arm and racquet extension during his serve.

An extensive list of what good players consider to be the most important "uptime" cues can be found in Appendix A.

Some Important
Questions and Answers

Since the price of this book does not include me, I've anticipated some of the questions the Sherlock Holmes Exercise might inspire:

Q: What am I supposed to see, hear, and feel?

A: Whatever you *do* see, hear, and feel. Each one of us has developed our own set of sensory cues that regulate our behavior; some have more than others. Also, some people become so involved as Sherlock, they think they're actually on the court; others simply remain aware of what's around them in the room. So don't go into this exercise with preconceived ideas.

Q: How come you had me change what I saw, heard, and felt so often? Why change colors to black-and-white and then back? Why change the tension in my muscles? Why change the volume of the sound?

A: Technically, I'm dealing with what we call *sensory sub-modalities* (see Appendix B). Modalities are seeing, hearing, and feeling. As you know, there are also the modalities of smelling and tasting, but they are of little consequence for our purposes. Submodalities are the refined elements of seeing, hearing, and feeling such as color, volume, and tension. When you vary the submodalities of sight, sound, and feeling, learning—and change—are most likely to occur.

Q: How do I determine the significance of all the internal and external A's, V's, and K's? There were so many that I don't know how to evaluate them.

A: Just make notes of the sights, sounds, and feelings that *seem* to be important. Postpone analyzing them. When you come to learning the various metaskills techniques later on, you can then decide which are the most useful.

Now that you know how to retrieve the details of past experience—the uptime and downtime A's, V's, and K's—let's start playing some of my mind games so your tennis game improves. If after doing the Sherlock Holmes Exercise you still have difficulty with re-creating images in your mind, recalling internal sounds, or feeling a variety of physical sensations, you can use the questions and exercises in Appendix B to expand and refine your sensory awareness. The better it is, the easier it will be for you to apply metaskills techniques.

THREE

Anchoring: Tapping Your Inner Resources

This chapter is your guide to making the most of your past experience. Here you'll learn how to identify the kinds of mental and emotional resources you have within you to play better tennis and then how to make them automatically available for eventual application on the court.

As you know, tennis is essentially a mental game, both because there's so much time to think in between shots and because tactical decisions are crucial to winning points. Only one third of a player's time is spent playing points. The other two thirds of match time are taken up with half-minute intervals between points, waiting for balls to be retrieved, and one-minute changeovers. The time for playing a point may last only eight to twelve seconds.

It's those between-point periods and changeovers that can jump up and jostle your mind. They can tense the muscles, decrease concentration, cause forgetfulness, reduce confidence, and eventually produce inconsistent shots—unless you know how to keep focused on the here and now.

What is needed, then, is a way to keep yourself in the

proper frame of mind between points, that is, in the appropriate emotional state when you're ready to rally. The appropriate states needed to play good tennis vary from person to person and situation to situation, depending perhaps on the score in points, games, or sets, the pace of play, and the ability of the opponent.

There are three underlying states of mind that are essential to playing well consistently. They are *concentration, confidence,* and a sense of *mind-body unity.* As you probably know, playing good tennis requires riveted concentration on the shot at hand. When not concentrating, many players either get ahead of themselves or drag the past into the point being played. Some players wish they were at the net instead of at the baseline; or they are thinking about the next set if they're too far behind in the present one. Others berate themselves for playing poorly as they usually do, thinking about past unforced errors that are being repeated in the match at hand. They forget that they still have a game to complete, a set or two to finish, and a point to play right now.

Confidence in your ability to execute a game plan and each shot well is necessary if you want to play your best. While in this state you know that a shot will be good even before you strike the ball. But when there's doubt in your mind, shots start to fly all over the place.

As a result of concentration and confidence, you will develop an inner sense of unity. This state of mind has elements of resonance and harmony, rhythmic energy, and grooved, coordinated movement that feels effortless. When in this state—some call it a "zone"—tennis players sense that their mind, mood, and movement are all of a piece, resulting in shots that are "pure." Their opponent's skill may still prevent them from winning; nevertheless, they have a sense of accomplishment in doing the best they know how.

Your Inner Resources

You've done a lot of living and have all sorts of resources stored in your memories that can be used to generate appropriate states of mind for playing good tennis. These resource states include, among others, optimism, eagerness, determination, calmness, inventiveness, hopefulness, acceptance, patience, friendliness, and a lot more. Optimism helps you think positively about your game; eagerness and determination keep you focused on the point at hand; calmness keeps your swing fluid after a stupid unforced error; inventiveness and hope are needed to execute new tactics; acceptance prevents frustration and anger from taking over when you make mistakes; patience allows you to wait for the opportunity to take advantage of your opponent's tendencies to make unforced errors; and friendliness allows you to overlook the ineptitude and perhaps the tennis ignorance of your opponents.

Other useful resources include past experiences related to learning all sorts of physical skills; embedded in these experiences are the basic resources for playing tennis well, such as balance, power, strength, energy, rhythm, coordination, and effort control. Finally, your past experiences of making good shots contain unconscious mental strategies, the resources that directly control your game.

Identifying the Right Resources

By now you've probably assumed that you're about to learn to put yourself into the right frame of mind—confident, optimistic, patient—at will. But first you must decide *which* resources to call up from your past experience. You'll know this by answering two basic questions:

- "Specifically, what kind of shots do I want to make?"

- "What stops me from executing my game plan and hitting the ball the way I'm capable of hitting it?"

First, knowing what you want comes from having alternatives in mind. These alternatives include remembering precisely when and how you've correctly implemented game plans and when and how you've hit similar shots in the past, remembering how other good players have applied similar tactics and similar shots, and recalling practice drills and instructions from your pro. This means knowing what you would have to see, hear, and feel to play the way you want to. When you know precisely what you want, you can transfer pertinent resources from past experiences to the kind of shots you want to make readily available.

Frequently the answer that people give to the second question is "I don't know. If I did, I'd do something about it." Yet there are ways to uncover the answer. One way is to guess. By guessing you'll be tapping into your unconscious mind, and guesses frequently turn out to be quite accurate.

If you have no good guesses, replay in your mind what you're doing incorrectly and compare it to the way you want to play, using your own past performance or someone else's performance as a standard for comparison. When you identify the difference between how you mentally regulate what you're actually doing on the court and how you mentally regulate what you want to do, you'll have some important clues as to what's stopping you.

Often it's your emotional state that stops you from playing good tennis. If you change to a just-right emotional state, your grooved shots—serves, topspins, slices, overheads, and volleys—will return. Consequently, by paying close attention to the mood you're in you may have the answer to what's stopping you. Perhaps you have been feeling annoyed, impatient, skeptical, despairing, or hopeless. After identifying this stopper state, all that's necessary is to replace it with its opposite.

This isn't always as easy as it may seem. Sometimes it might be impossible to discover all the factors that keep you from achieving your desired outcomes. You may need the help of a tennis professional to refine the mechanics of your strokes, or you might profit from the help of a skilled counselor, to deal with unconscious conflicts that could interfere with maintaining the mood you need to play well.

Nonetheless, knowing how to identify and use your internal resources is a valuable process in itself; so let's look at it now.

Accessing Internal Resources

Fortunately NLP has formalized the normal human process of tapping past experiences and making them automatically available for use in present situations. The Sherlock Holmes Exercise is part of this process; you already know it. You'll be pleasantly surprised to discover that by reliving past experiences in full detail you have more resources for playing better tennis than you thought you had. When you discover this, you'll trust yourself more and build your self-confidence.

Anchoring is another part of the process that makes your internal resources—your past experiences and feelings, still available to you in your subconscious—automatically available to play better tennis in spite of conditions that conspire to make the game difficult. Anchors keep your resources stabilized so your game can become more consistent and enjoyable. Let's turn to the process of anchoring in general. Later you'll learn how to use a variety of anchors for specific aspects of your game.

What Is an Anchor?

I am reasonably certain that you already know what an anchor is and how it works, but you may not know that you know. It is either an internal or an actual external sight, sound, feeling, smell, or taste—a stimulus—that triggers the sensory details associated with a particular past experience. When you see an old photograph of yourself as a child, it usually stirs up memories of that time in your life. Similarly, when you hear airplanes overhead and see tens of thousands of people surrounding the stadium court, you could think of the U.S. Open. It's the same with a special song.

It's a fact that our conscious and unconscious thoughts—what we see, hear, feel, smell, and taste internally—directly affect our moods or internal emotional states. Consequently, we can become conditioned to respond emotionally in the same way over and over again whenever we generate a particular thought or whenever a particular stimulus is experienced. You may vaguely remember hearing this from someone else: Pavlov, who got the dog to salivate simply by ringing a bell.

Our lives are full of anchors, some of which have powerful effects. The sight of the American flag or the sound of "America the Beautiful" inspires deep feelings of patriotism in some people. Seeing a snake or spider can evoke intense fear in those who are phobic. The smell of popcorn stirs up just-right feelings that make Peter Carruthers, a 1984 Olympic pairs skater, skate his best. The thought of a past event—like putting away a lob to win a match—can evoke the same feelings associated with it in the here and now.

Tennis players have more anchors than the Sixth Fleet. Unfortunately most of them are negative, similar to phobias. Serving the first ball, for instance, is enough to create intense anxiety in many players. Even the thought of participating in a tournament can evoke discomfort in some people or arouse excited anticipation in others. Second serves during tiebreakers seem to evoke gloom or fear in some players. All an uncertain player has to do is prepare for the second serve, and he gets visions of the ball either being netted or floating over the net to be put away as a winner by his opponent.

Other anchors consist of some form of conscious, compulsive, and superstitious behavior. Superstitious anchors range from wearing certain pieces of jewelry or clothing for good luck to believing in a "trusty" racquet that is expected to produce victory every time. Some players either step on the baseline or avoid stepping on it deliberately to bring them good luck on the next point.

All of these conscious, uncontrollable phobic responses and compulsive, ritualistic behaviors override the ability to make intelligent choices about your actions. Conscious ritualistic behaviors include bouncing the ball exactly nine times before each serve and wiping your racquet with a towel after each point; their use can create internal pressure and distract you from absorbing important external information, such as your opponent's state of fatigue or the strength of the wind that could affect the ball's flight. Moreover, they interfere with the internal state that is most appropriate for executing well-placed tennis shots.

On the other hand, metaskills anchors automatically evoke good feelings, without the need for conscious thought; they utilize your talents and emotional states so that you play well consistently. This frees you to enjoy the game and your playing companions.

Retrieving Past Experiences

Let's see how we can use the Sherlock Holmes Exercise to retrieve past experiences so they can be anchored for practical use while playing tennis. In that exercise you learned how to go inside your mind and retrieve or remember a past experience. You learned how to run your brain by modifying sights, sounds, and feelings. And you identified the condition or state of consciousness when your mental thoughts, emotions, and muscles conspired to hit as fine a tennis shot as you had ever made.

This process of "going inside"—remembering what you saw, heard, and felt during a particular past experience—is, as I've said, central to practically all of my mind games. It's there, in your brain and muscles, that you have all the resources you need to play tennis as well as your physical condition and skills will allow or to do anything else worth doing.

Sherlock Holmes Revisited

Let's revisit the Sherlock Holmes Exercise as a way to learn how to anchor. Quickly reread the instructions on page 22 of Chapter 2. When you've finished reading, go inside and go back to that wonderful shot that you examined as Sherlock Holmes before. See, hear, and feel again what you saw, heard, and felt when you hit that shot. Be sure to make regular pictures, not metapictures, because regular pictures elicit stronger feelings. Especially feel the emotions you felt *while* you were hitting it. Pay attention to the bodily sensations of that emotional state. Perhaps it's a tingling feeling, goose bumps, warmth, a rush of blood, a feeling of energy or power in some part of your body.

As you become aware of these sensations, press one

finger against any *one specific part of your body*. Increase the
amount of finger pressure as the intensity of the emotional
sensations increases; as they subside, reduce the amount of
finger pressure. That's the anchor—a K-anchor—the pressure
of your finger on a specific part of your body. The central idea
is to associate the anchor with the emotional feeling.

When the emotional feeling is at its most intense level, let
one, and only one, internal image associated with the shot
flash *spontaneously* into your mind; then let one sound
associated with the shot pop *spontaneously* into your head.
The image and sound are also anchors—a V-anchor and an
A-anchor. They should be related directly and specifically to
the past shot and not to tennis in general.

Now let your mind go blank and come back to the present.
Take a 5- or 10-minute break from reading this book and do
something else to distract your mind from what you have
been reading. At the end of the break, return to this point in
the book.

Welcome back. Take a moment to determine the nature of
the state you're in right now. After that, press your finger on
the exact same spot on your body when you were Sherlock.
Hold the finger pressure for a full 60 seconds without reading
any further than the end of this paragraph. Just pay attention
to what happens inside, nothing else, and then return to the
book when the 60 seconds are up.

Welcome back again. Are you thinking about the past good
shot? Do you now see or hear what you saw or heard then?
Do you now feel the same emotions you felt when you hit that
shot? I'd be surprised if you aren't aware of some aspect of
the shot, assuming you followed my instructions. If you
reactivated some of the same feelings, images, or sounds
associated with the shot, you have experienced how an
anchor works. Within 60 seconds you changed your state.

Now reflect on the meaning of this experience. Do you realize that you can change your state quickly and therefore don't have to stay stuck in a lousy state? With a properly established anchor you have more choices about the way you want to feel, and you can activate any state automatically if your anchor is "contextualized."

Contextual Anchors

If an anchored resource is to be useful on the tennis court, it must be contextualized; that is, the anchor should fire *automatically*, without conscious thought, in the context of a special situation when a particular resource is needed, not just at any old time or in any situation. If anxiety normally takes over on the first serve, a confidence anchor could be triggered automatically just before you set up at the baseline. If you want to keep your cool when your opponent stalls, a calmness anchor could be activated automatically when you first notice the stall. If a delicate drop shot is required, the anchored feeling of having a fine touch could be fired automatically as you approach and make contact with the ball.

When you contextualize an anchor, it's important to select either a movement, an *external* visual cue, or an *external* auditory cue that is always present on the tennis court to serve as an anchor. Only one cue is necessary. For example, taking your racquet out of its case, a K-anchor, could be an anchor for generating the resource of determination; looking at the center tab, a V-anchor, could be used to get into the right state for serving.

Your ingenuity is all that's necessary to identify an anchor. Using as an anchor a habitual, unconscious movement that occurs in a particular situation or context is most effective since it already is unconsciously automatic. Habitual, unconscious movements could include the way you hold the racquet with both hands when playing at the net, a gesture of a hand or an arm as you prepare for an overhead, or the crouch position you take when preparing to receive a serve.

The only limitation on your choice of an anchor is that it be "clean"—not already associated with an experience on or off the tennis court. For example, looking at a wedding ring would not be a good V-anchor because it's already connected to very powerful emotional experiences.

Making Anchors
Work Automatically

To establish these anchors fully so they'll be useful later on, it's necessary to "fire" them consciously three or four times a day for a week or two, until the anchored emotional state is activated within a few seconds. Then forget about conscious anchoring, letting the process become part of your unconscious mind. The act of firing an anchor consists of deliberately looking at an external visual cue, or listening to an external sound cue, or moving in a habitual way, while associating the cue or movement with the actual emotional feeling of a resourceful state.

If you would like to *establish* the finger-pressing anchor related to the good shot that you identified as Sherlock, press your finger on the specific part of your body and consciously see the internal image and hear the internal sound that were part of the remembered shot. The finger pressure should be maintained until you feel the return of the full force of the emotional sensations you had while hitting that past shot. Repeat this process several times each day for the next week or two. With this anchor-firing practice you'll eventually be able to reactivate the emotional state associated with the past shot in a matter of seconds.

If you want to contextualize the anchor for that past good shot, select either a habitual movement, an *external* visual cue, or an *external* auditory cue that is always present on the tennis court to serve as a new, substitute anchor. Practice firing this new anchor three or four times a day for several weeks until it works as well as the finger pressure; this may be done on or off the court. When you're off the court, just think about the external cue or make the habitual movement until you can produce the emotional state in a few seconds.

One professional tennis player looks at the printed logo on his racquet; it's his V-anchor for generating determination. Another player looks at the end of the grip on his racquet; this is his V-anchor to activate a state of concentration. A third player listens to the rhythmic sound of his feet as he walks to the baseline between shots; this A-anchor returns him to a feeling of calmness after he makes a poor shot.

Each of these players used finger pressure on some part of their body when they first identified and anchored their resource during the Sherlock Holmes Exercise. They fired the finger-pressure anchor on the tennis court to regenerate the desired state. Then they transferred the feeling anchored by the finger pressure to a new A-, V-, or K-anchor that is always present on the court.

The players practiced firing these new anchors both on and off the court. When at home or in the office, they imagined they were on the court. Then they saw, heard, or felt their particular anchor and consciously generated their desired emotional state. After they were able to generate the desired state in association with a particular anchor within a matter of seconds, they stopped formal practice and allowed their unconscious minds to take over—just the way hearing a certain song can automatically generate a feeling of love for a special person.

ANCHORING

1. Identify the resource needed to achieve a desired outcome or to execute a particular shot.

2. Remember a past experience when you used that resource successfully.

3. "Go inside" and see, hear, and feel again what you saw, heard, and felt during that past resourceful experience.

4. Intensify the internal, emotional feelings that were present during (not after) the time when you were actively involved in accomplishing a particular outcome or executing a particular shot.

5. Anchor the internal, emotional feelings or state with finger pressure and with an image and sound that were directly associated with that past experience.

6. Contextualize the anchor to a sight, sound, touch, or habitual movement that will always be present in the tennis environment.

7. Practice firing the anchor four or five times per day for about two or three weeks so that the internal, emotional feelings can be regenerated within a matter of a few seconds.

Now that you know how to anchor a resource, you'll learn the practical uses of anchors in subsequent chapters.

II

Metaskills
Techniques

Now that you are aware of your mental detective skills—the tools of sensory awareness—you're ready to uncover your internal resources and apply them to improve your tennis game. The metaskills mind games in this part of the book are designed to allow you to (1) identify and stabilize in your mind and body the just-right states that make for consistent play, (2) discover how to take advantage of the pro within yourself, (3) expand your ability to use the power of self-hypnosis, and (4) learn how to control pain, unleash stored energy, and speed up healing so you can play at your physical best. In short, you'll be learning mind games to control your tennis game.

Read through this section of the book leisurely. When you discover a technique that fits a goal you have in mind, put it to work. *Follow the instructions precisely.* Evaluate the effectiveness of the technique: did you achieve a desired outcome?

If you're not sure about the application of a particular technique, go to the last section, "Game, Set, Match." This section, along with Appendix C, will help you select appropriate techniques to achieve your desired outcomes.

FOUR

Just-Right State: Concentration

There's a special racquet that successful tennis players use. They use it just before the start of each point. You can't serve a ball with it or even see it. Call it mood—the state you take to the court that determines how you serve yourself and the returns you get from it.

The mood or emotional state that you take onto the court determines how effectively you apply your game plan. That mood can change as quickly as lightning strikes, depending on your values and how your mind works, consciously and unconsciously.

Some days you're hot. Shots fly so true that they land millimeters inside the lines as if guided by lasers. Open spaces on the opponent's court are spotlighted and all but announce where your next out-of-reach shot should be placed. Invisible magnets attract all the net-cord shots—yours and your opponent's—so they fall on *his* side of the net.

On other days you feel heat of a different sort. You're hot under the collar. You're so frustrated you can't even hit the floor with your hat. Glaciers hustle along faster than it takes your opponent to serve. Somehow the slightest breeze turns your returns into sitters or wafts them yards behind the baseline. You don't know whether, as the country song goes, to shoot yourself or go bowling.

Mood swings are as important as the way you swing your racquet, and your mind controls both. Fortunately you don't have to be the victim of your not-so-good states; you can either maintain a good state or quickly change it from lousy to just right. You can learn to make all the between-point and changeover time work to quiet your mind and to have all the necessary mental and physical resources readily and automatically available for executing your game plan and making superb shots. If you don't, the fun of tennis could regress into a state of emotional self-deprecation.

In Part I you learned how to use your mind to access your inner resources. This chapter and the next two deal with the process of using your mind and inner resources to control and change your moods since they dramatically affect the way you play.

If you're a highly ranked international player, and you commit six straight unforced errors in the fifth set, down 3–4, there *is* a way to keep utter frustration from boiling over during the next couple of games. I'll teach you how to uncover and regain your feelings of confidence so that you can perform comfortably at the peak of your capacity when the chips are down. In essence you'll learn how to get into the just-right states that are conducive to playing all sorts of points well, using the anchoring process described in Chapter 3.

A few tour players use a natural, unconscious process of anchoring just-right states. Ivan Lendl, for example, picks at the strings of his racquet as a means of readying himself for the next point, and Steffi Graf slaps her left thigh repeatedly after making an error as a way to step up her concentration and determination.

In each of these cases Ivan and Steffi "fire" their anchors automatically, without conscious thought. They just find themselves doing it. And I'm reasonably certain that you have an anchor or two tucked away in your unconscious mind that work for you.

I have developed several step-by-step anchoring processes that you can use to get and keep yourself in the just-right state for hitting each shot facing you at the moment. These anchors evolved from my systematic study of what athletes in many different sports do to generate and stabilize their moods. I refer to them generally as *just-right anchors*.

All just-right anchors have the same basic steps, but there are some slight differences in their development and application. The basic steps were presented in Chapter 3. In addition to direct recall of emotional states associated with past resourceful experiences, I use music, color, and metaphorical images to access appropriate resources and to stabilize just-right states. As you study these metaskills techniques, you may find several of them more to your liking than others.

For convenience I've grouped these anchoring techniques into three categories that represent the three underlying states—concentration, confidence, and mind-body unity. This chapter focuses on concentration. The next two chapters will deal with confidence and getting into the "zone" respectively.

As strange as it seems, the epitome of concentration is paying attention to absolutely nothing. Some tennis pros accidentally stumble onto this principle. For example, when Zina Garrison defeated Navratilova in the 1988 U.S. Open quarterfinals, she said, "I lost the score. I didn't know what it was. When I was 4–2, I thought it was 2–1. I think it [not thinking] helped more than anything. I just played the ball."

For every tennis player at every level, thinking about not thinking is close to impossible. We'll start by whittling tennis thoughts down to one per shot. It isn't as hard to achieve as it might seem. The one thought, what I call a *cue* or a *key,* is the thing that helps trigger a rhythmic effort. The choice of the right cue is based partly, as you might have guessed, on the form of sensory information easiest for you to process— auditory, visual, or kinesthetic—while you're playing a shot at hand. It's also based on what works.

In my own case, for example, when I pay sole attention to increasing racquet speed at impact, a K-cue, my arms become tense and I hurry the stroke; I end up losing what I want: power and control. However, if I concentrate on seeing the racquet hit the back of the ball, a V-cue, my stroke is satisfactory and provides lots of power. Although both of these cues are important to a good tennis stroke, only one is helpful to me. Only I could have discovered that, just as only you can sift out which uptime cues are most useful for you.

Uptime Anchor

The uptime anchor is one metaskills technique that will help you identify the most useful cues for you. When you've identified them, you can decide which ones, when attended to one at a time, will elicit your most intensive level of concentration.

An average club player—I'll call him Scott—wanted to improve his concentration. He was utterly confused by having to pay attention to too many keys. He'd gotten lots of advice from pros and books but couldn't distinguish what was important.

"Let's work on hitting a topspin forehand down the line," he told me one afternoon during a practice session with a practice partner.

"Hit a few balls down the line and pay attention to what you become aware of *naturally* as you approach and hit each ball," I said. "Move to the ball, get set, and hit it without giving yourself directions, sort of mindlessly, and notice whatever you see, hear, or feel on the outside."

After Scott hit 8 or 10 shots, I asked him what he *saw* on the outside that seemed useful. He mentioned his hands and feet, the racquet moving back, the ball, the net cord, his opponent's position on the court. These are all potentially useful cues for Scott.

"Fine," I said, "and what did you *feel?*" Once again, I wanted him to notice *external* feelings—on the skin and in his muscles and joints. I told him to scan his body for muscle tension in all the important parts of his racquet preparation and stroke, such as the grip with his hands; the movement of his arms, shoulders, and hips during the backswing; and the leg and hip action while shifting his weight.

Scott said he felt his fingers on the racquet, turning his shoulders, the wind in his face, the forward momentum of his body after he made contact with the ball, and, oh yes, a slippery spot on the court.

"And what did you *hear?*"

"Not too much, except the truck in the background, the sound of the ball hitting my racquet strings, my sneakers squeaking on the court. Yeah, when I heard the truck, the shot wasn't very good."

I said I wanted him to hit a few topspin forehands while paying attention to only *one* of those sensory cues at a time. He first chose shifting his weight—a K-cue. Before he hit the ball, I wondered what he thought would be an acceptable performance on a scale of 1 to 10.

"About an eight or a nine."

"You're too tough on yourself, like a lot of players," I said. "Lendl doesn't hit them all perfectly, remember, and you're a club player."

He settled on seven.

"Okay, go ahead and hit a few balls while paying strict attention to the action that controls your weight shift as you stroke the ball. Nothing else. And concentrate on that action throughout the *entire* process."

Scott hit about six or seven balls, all but two of which were at least seventh heaven. Two were better than sevens, and one, he felt, was as pure as he could hit a forehand topspin, a solid, perfect 10.

"I can't believe I hit the ball so well," he said, also admitting that he'd lost concentration on two shots that went way out of court.

"Let's anchor the feelings of making those good shots in relation to paying attention to your weight shift," I said. "This uptime anchor is a process of associating one cue with the physical feelings of *the entire swing*. We'll use a visual anchor, a part of your body or piece of equipment you'll always have with you."

Scott chose a small scar on the back of his hand.

"Not a good idea," I said. "An anchor should be 'clean.' By that I mean something that's not already associated with an experience of yours. Your scar is probably connected to a painful injury, which makes the scar 'dirty' for my purposes."

"Yeah, I got the scar when I ran into a net post a few years ago. That was a bummer. How about looking at the logo on my racquet? It's always visible."

"Fine. This is how I want you to create the anchor. First, remember all the physical sensations of hitting those good forehand topspins—the muscle tension and the mechanics involved in the preparation and execution of the shots and your weight shift while stroking the ball."

Scott looked out ahead while swinging his racquet gently, nodded, and said he was getting it.

"Now, as you look at the logo, say to yourself, 'I'm storing in the logo the feeling of hitting topspin forehands while paying attention to my weight shift.' Put those swing feelings into your logo."

"Whaaaaat?" Scott was not comfortable talking to a logo.

"Humor me," I said. "Pretend you're storing all the muscle feelings and movements you used during those shots in your racquet logo." Scott peered at the logo for about 10 seconds, then said, "Okay, now what?"

I asked how he'd done it, how he'd stored the feelings of shifting his weight in such an unfamiliar way.

"I used a mental laser beam and projected a good shot into it," he replied.

"And the feelings of the weight shift? Did you store all of them too?"

"As I was zapping the logo with my laser, I was feeling the entire stroke," he told me, "*especially* the weight shift."

I told Scott to choose another cue, something he had *seen*. He chose the position of his hand on the racquet and concentrated on it while hitting another half a dozen shots.

Most of the shots were lousy. Fives at best. Not worth anchoring.

He picked another V-cue, watching the ball strike his racquet strings. This time his practice shots were up to his standard of excellence. I had him "stack" that cue into the logo.

We experimented like this for quite a while, picking cues he thought important and then hitting shots with only them in his mind. Some he rejected; some he anchored. I told him to

identify and anchor uptime cues for other specific shots—
backhands, volleys, overheads, serves, half volleys.

Near the end of the process Scott asked, "When and how
do I fire this anchor?"

"The only time I want you to fire it," I replied, "is when you
lose concentration while playing, when you find yourself
thinking about too many things, and when you're not hitting
the ball well. And the way to fire it is to merely look at the
logo and say, 'Okay, unconscious mind, take over.'"

"How will that make me concentrate?"

"Concentration is paradoxical. The less you think about,
the more you concentrate. Honest. And the better you'll hit
tennis balls. You'll be as good as your body and ability allow.
You just demonstrated this principle while you were building
the anchor.

"You were able to hit fine shots while concentrating on only
one cue. That meant your unconscious mind was attending to
all the rest of the stuff that made the shots good. It was free
to do that because your conscious mind was not interfering.

"You were in what a pro friend of mine, Lenny Scheuermann, calls the 'now' state. Firing the anchor puts you back
into that state."

I told Scott to make sure he understood the difference
between practice and playing. Practice was for concentrating
on only one of his important cues at a time: five minutes for
weight shift, five minutes for watching the ball, and so on.

"When you're in a match," I said, "just play. Get into that
'now' state and stay there."

The uptime anchor may not be for you if you're a highly
skilled player. It could be more distracting than helpful, for
you're already skilled at paying unconscious attention to the
details of preparing for and hitting each shot.

UPTIME ANCHOR

1. Select a part of your body or equipment that will serve as a "clean" V-anchor.

2. Identify the particular shot you want to improve (forehand, net volley, serve).

3. Identify the *external* auditory (A), visual (V), and kinesthetic (K) cues that you notice while executing a particular shot during practice. (See Appendix A for cues that others believe to be important.)

4. Execute the shot about six times, paying attention to one, *and only one*, sensory cue, and rate each on a scale of 1 to 10.

5. Anchor the mechanical feelings of making a satisfactory shot, not the emotional feelings you had about its quality.

6. Do this by looking at your anchor and saying: "I'm storing the mechanical feelings of making [fill in the shot] in relation to paying attention to [such-and-such cue]."

7. Repeat steps 4–6 for each external visual, auditory, and kinesthetic cue. This is "stacking."

8. Repeat steps 4–7 for each kind of shot.

9. Build the anchor over two to three weeks. To fire it, look at the specific anchor spot for about 60 seconds and say: "Okay, unconscious mind, take over!"

Note: This is a process mostly for average players and beginners. Highly ranked players should pass this one by.

Mechanical
Just-Right Anchor

Another way to increase your concentration is by using a mechanical just-right anchor. It consists of making an internal, metaphorical picture that represents either your entire swing or parts of it. This kind of image tends to distract the conscious mind from paying direct attention to too many parts of the swing.

My friend Lenny Scheuermann, one of the finer young teaching pros, suggests using the image of an airplane gently gliding onto a runway when hitting an underspin backhand. A client of mine thinks of a candy cane to guide her backswing and hitting stroke on forehand shots. Chet Murphy, internationally known tennis teacher, suggests the image of "honoring the flag," that is, placing the racquet hand across the chest when hitting backhand volleys.

These particular images might work for you. You can test their usefulness. Ones that you develop yourself will probably be better. In any case the following are instructions for creating a mechanical just-right anchor.

MECHANICAL
JUST-RIGHT ANCHOR

1. Practice.

2. Practice some more.

3. When you're executing a practice shot, let an image pop into your mind that represents the way you want the entire tennis stroke or parts of it to look (e.g., racquet back, shoulder turn, weight shifts, etc.).

4. Hit several balls to determine whether the shot stays fine with that spontaneous image.

5. Reinforce that V-anchor by hitting three or four of those particular shots several times a week for a week or two.

6. Reinforce the V-anchor, off the court, several times a day for about a week. Visualize candy canes, airplanes, or whatever, at home or at the office. If anyone should inquire about the smile on your face, hand him this book.

7. After completing step 6, let your unconscious mind take over. Do nothing more.

FIVE

Just-Right State: Confidence

A common desired outcome of all tennis players is to be confident that they can carry out their game plans and execute most of the shots as they arise. It's the same as the common desire of all humans to catch the next available whiff of air. Confidence in tennis is a bit tougher than breathing—it comes with experience.

To build their confidence many players say to themselves, "I've played well in the past, so I can play well today." However, merely saying that is not enough to establish a lasting state of confidence. Generalizations about past performance don't work. What's needed to become confident is automatic and repeated generation of *specific* memories of hitting good shots. Here is one metaskills technique you can use to produce a genuine feeling of confidence.

Tennis Resource Anchor

I helped one touring professional build his confidence and access the just-right states for hitting several kinds of specific shots. He used an anchoring technique that involved "stacking." An anchor is stacked when you associate more than one idea or feeling with it.

Scott, my club player, wanted to make his first service more consistent. Missing his first serve eroded his confidence. He had already determined that one of his mechanical "keys" for serving well was putting pressure on the racquet handle with the last three fingers of his right hand. To remind himself to have a firm grip at impact, he would deliberately and *routinely* squeeze those fingers *during his preparation* for all serves. That squeeze became his anchor for serving.

As we stood at the service line, I told him to determine where he wanted the ball to land in the opponent's court and to remember a past successful first service that he had made when the match was tight. He had had many such experiences over the years, so it wasn't difficult.

Scott took his normal stance with his left foot an inch or so behind the baseline, racquet held so that it was pointed downward and forward at about a 60-degree angle to the ground.

"Now, I want you to *be very precise about remembering* and anchoring that past service," I said. "See, hear, and feel what you saw, heard, and felt then until you become aware of the emotional state you were in *while* you were serving the ball, not the feelings after you hit it." How he felt *after* a successful shot is obvious—and useless.

It took Scott a few moments, but then he said, "I've got it. I was really determined to get the ball into the back left corner of the service court. I felt like I couldn't miss."

"How do you know you felt determined?" I asked. "What sensations in your body let you know you felt determined? Really pay attention to sensations that indicate determination—in your shoulders, chest, stomach, arms, wherever."

"My chest was full, like I was able to take deep breaths and had lots of air in my lungs," he said. "When I'm determined to play well, I get that full feeling a lot."

"Before anchoring that feeling," I said, "let's do a prior test of its usefulness. Generate that feeling strongly right now and in your mind serve a ball to where you want it to go in the opponent's service court. As you make that serve mentally, find out if the ball goes the way you want it to, in both its speed and its trajectory."

I told him that if his mental serve wasn't up to his required level of performance he was to select another prior service, identify the emotional state associated with it, and test it before anchoring. In this instance he said his mental shot turned out just fine.

Continuing, I said, "Anchor that feeling of determination in your chest by squeezing your last three fingers on the racquet as you hold the racquet down at your side. Match the amount of finger squeeze with the amount of determination you feel in your chest as you relive that previous serve."

I told him to *prepare for this present serve as he normally would* and to generate the feeling of determination by squeezing his fingers on the racquet, releasing the squeeze as soon as he felt determined. I emphasized that he should prepare to serve as he always had, applying no more or less pressure on the racquet than normal, and then serve *without any thought whatsoever.* Just serve the ball.

The serve hit the lines at the corner of the service court. Then I had Scott evaluate the quality of his serving movement again to make sure the emotional state of determination from the prior shot was just right.

"That's exactly the serve I had in mind," Scott said. "I had the same feeling of determination, too. That's what I want every time."

We repeated the process for several other kinds of serves to both the ad and deuce courts, each time "stacking" other emotional feelings associated with past first serves into the same K-anchor—squeezing the last three fingers of the right hand on the racquet.

In essence Scott created a *contextualized anchor*—a *physical movement that he naturally uses every time* he prepares to serve. After he established the anchor with repeated practice during the following weeks, it fired automatically because it was a part of his normal preparatory routine.

I repeated the entire anchoring process with different kinds of shots—forehand and backhand ground strokes, overheads, half volleys, net play, drop shots. He created a *new K-anchor for each kind of shot:* "stutter" steps while getting ready for overheads, placement of his left hand on the throat of the racquet as he prepared for volleying at the net, knees bent for half volleys, and bending from the waist while waiting to return service. All of them were natural movements that Scott normally made *during his preparation* for each kind of shot. He anchored or mentally associated emotions related to previous shots made in similar circumstances with those natural movements.

When we were finished, I asked him what he had learned from the process.

"I've learned I could recall past shots quite fast once I got the hang of it," he said. "When I was in the right state, I found I wasn't brooding over shots the way I used to. I was too busy making the shot at hand."

Scott had one question: Was he supposed to do this anchoring process every time he practiced? If so, he worried that his playing partners would become bored or impatient with his repetition.

I suggested that he share his knowledge about anchoring with his fellow players and that they alternate building their anchors, spending about 15 minutes each on the process as part of their prematch warm-up routine. After about 10–15 practice sessions he would have stacked enough feelings of confidence in executing practically all the different tennis shots. And by that time the anchors would fire automatically, leaving him free to develop new shots.

"When do I fire each of these anchors?" he asked.

"Only during practice as you're building them," I replied. "Practice firing each of them both on and off the court several times a day for two or three weeks; they'll become automatic during matches. When the states associated with each type of shot are generated in a matter of seconds after firing them, stop the anchor-building process and let your unconscious mind do the rest. You know, like Pavlov's dog salivating when the bell rings."

"And what if I'm faced with an opponent who causes me to question my confidence? What do I do then?" he asked. "Do I fire all of these anchors while I'm playing?"

"Hold the phone," I told him. "We'll get to that in a few minutes. Let's finish this process first. Then we'll talk about how to get yourself into the right competitive state. All we're doing now is working on each shot, making them consistent."

The following is an outline of the steps involved in creating your own just-right anchors for various tennis shots. Essentially you'll be anchoring confidence in being able to consistently execute many different shots, time after time.

TENNIS RESOURCE ANCHOR

1. When you're ready to practice a particular kind of shot (serve, overhead, backhand, topspin, etc.), remember a specific time and place *during a match* when you executed that kind of shot very well.

2. Go inside and see, hear, and feel again what you saw, heard, and felt then.

3. Remember the physical sensations of executing the prior shot *and* the emotional state you experienced *as you were executing it.*

4. Mentally play the shot you're practicing and evaluate the effectiveness of the prior emotional state before you anchor it.

5. Anchor the emotional feelings with a unique and *natural movement* that is part of your normal *preparatory routine* for that kind of shot.

6. After you have generated the emotional feelings of the prior shot, practice hitting that type of shot six to eight times.

7. Practice firing the anchor three or four times a day for two or three weeks—at home, in the office, on the court, wherever. By then you should be playing on automatic pilot.

The same process can be used for each type of tennis shot. The result is that you will have about six or seven different just-right resource anchors that will eventually fire automatically during competition. If you discover that a particular shot is becoming inconsistent, you can repeat the seven-step process and create a new anchor for it during your practice sessions.

Scott and I spent a lot of time building his just-right resource anchors. He had the luxury of belonging to a club and had lots of time to practice. So, what do you do if you're a public-court player who is limited to perhaps 45 minutes? About all I can say is that you could play matches once or twice a week and use the other court time for practice.

Competitive-State Anchor

There are times during competition when anxious moments unnerve even the most highly skilled players. Often the anxiety is a manifestation of a lack of confidence in one's ability, if only at certain times during a match. As most players know, when we lack confidence, especially at the opening of a match and at crucial points and games, our ability to hit the ball often goes kerflooey. Quick recovery from these periodic episodes of self-doubt is crucial to enjoying tennis and playing well. What's necessary is to be competition-keen and stay that way. An anchor can help you do that.

A competitive-state anchor can be created by playing in your mind a complete and successful tennis match against a particular opponent (on the tournament court) the day or night before a match. This means that you know the tendencies of your opponent to play in certain ways under certain conditions and that you have developed a game plan to take advantage of your opponent's strong and weak points.

The idea is to play a fantasy match with your opponent, mentally executing as many different and difficult shots as might occur during the actual match. As you mentally execute successful shots, anchor the positive feelings generated during the fantasy round by stacking them into *one* anchor while you're playing the mind match. The anchor can be an ordinary movement like stroking your chin, rubbing your arm, or pulling your ear.

If, in your mind, a shot doesn't turn out right, replay it several times until it does. If a particular shot continues to be troublesome in your fantasy, never mind. Continue playing the mind match, anchoring the good feelings. Later, after the match is over, you can devote practice time to correcting the errant fantasy shot. If it occurs in the match, so be it.

When you are finished, you will have anchored (stacked) good feelings of confidence many times, and you will have mentally reviewed the match in advance. Practice firing this one competitive-state anchor several times until it generates confidence in a matter of seconds.

When you first arrive at the tournament grounds, and as you approach your assigned court, fire the competitive-state anchor. If you become overly anxious while playing, fire the competitive-state anchor during the changeover to swing you back to a better frame of mind.

COMPETITIVE-STATE ANCHOR

1. Fantasize playing a complete match on the tournament court against a specific opponent.

2. Anchor and stack the feelings of making good shots and the confidence associated with each of them. Use a normal gesture as your anchor.

3. Practice firing the anchor until you can access your state of confidence within a few seconds.

4. Fire the anchor prior to the start of a match and during changeovers when you feel *overly* uncertain during competition.

Personal Power

Playing a successful fantasy match before a tournament and anchoring feelings of confidence may not overcome more pervasive feelings of insecurity. Sometimes anxiety starts hours or perhaps days before a tournament begins, manifested in stomach discomfort and headaches. Sometimes insecurity begins to gnaw at a player's mind toward the end of a tournament, when he or she reaches the round of 16. If you haven't developed ways to cope with your anxiety, you may perform poorly at crucial times during many tournaments. Moreover, your feelings of insecurity can also affect other parts of your life, such as school, work, and social relationships.

There's a way, however, to tap your resources of powerful effectiveness; it's a process I've developed that keeps you in touch with your feelings of competence and confidence so you can perform comfortably at the peak of your capacity when the chips are down. It's a personal power anchor—an anchor to be used sparingly and for only the most significant events in your life.

I hit upon this idea of anchoring personal power after thinking about what Carlos Castaneda wrote in his book *Journey to Ixtlan* (Simon and Schuster, 1972, pp. 181–189). Don Juan, Carlos's sorcerer, talked about the importance of

being prepared to face fear and death gracefully and courageously. He said that each person should identify a personal
place of power—an actual geographical place where he has
experienced a sense of awe combined with exhilaration,
strength, and confidence.

Whenever that person reaches a goal of utmost significance, he is to return to his place of power, either in actuality
or in fantasy, and "deposit" the feelings of powerful effectiveness there. Then, according to Don Juan, when death
approaches over his left shoulder, he is to return to his place
of power, either in actuality or in fantasy, gather the
deposited power into his being, and dance the dance of
death—that is, face death courageously, replacing the feelings of fear with power.

Don Juan created a process to deal with death; I have
converted it to deal with living. My process, the personal
power anchor, consists of identifying your place of power,
"storing" the feelings associated with your own experiences
of being powerfully competent, and eventually tapping those
resources of power when you're faced with events of utmost
significance in your life, which are sometimes frightening or
anxiety-provoking. Essentially the process is an anchor
that you fire to empower yourself to make living full of
rich experiences instead of anxious ones. Here's how it
works.

Identify a
Personal Place of Power

In your mind, go back to a specific time and place—a place
that overwhelmed you with its beauty, where you were at
one with nature and the universe, where you experienced a
sense of excitement and confidence. That place may be close
by or hundreds of miles away. It could be in the mountains,

near a lake or the ocean, in the midst of a forest or a field of grass, under a majestic tree, next to a cool stream, in the rain or snow—no matter, just a very special place for you.

Go inside and see, hear, and feel what you saw, heard, and felt when you were in that place. Notice the light, shadows, and colors; listen to the pitch, volume, and tone of the sounds; and especially feel the sensations of awe, excitement, and confidence that you felt while in that special place. That special place is going to be where you, in your imagination, can "store" all the feelings you've had when you did things superbly, powerfully, and independently. It's also a place where you can eventually store all of the feelings of powerful competence that you'll experience in the future.

Identify Past Experiences of Power

Remember and relive a time in your life when you performed a task, any task, superbly. Perhaps you felt a sense of graceful and easy power as you played your very best tennis. You might have felt extremely satisfied after giving a fine speech before a large audience. You might have been excited after completing a top-notch interview. You might have been really pleased after playing a part in a school or college play. Or you might have had a deep feeling of caring and love after writing a letter to a special person.

Relive that past experience of powerful effectiveness. See, hear, and feel again what you saw, heard, and felt then. See the things you saw on the inside—in your mind—and on the outside. Pay close attention to the submodalities; *most of all,* feel those physical sensations of powerful effectiveness and confidence.

Anchor the Powerful
Experience with a K-Anchor

As a K-anchor, use a movement that is natural and unobtrusive, such as touching your face or making a fist. Associate the K-anchor with a special image and sound that are directly related to the past experience.

Create a
Storehouse of Power

Fire the K-anchor, and when the feelings of power are strong, "deposit" those feelings in the one particular spot you have chosen as your personal place of power. In your mind metaphorically see that power stored there.

Increase the amount of stored power by repeating the same process with other past experiences of achievement. Continue to build your storehouse of power when you have similar experiences in the future. "Stack" feelings of power from each new experience into the *same* K-anchor.

Tap the
Storehouse of Power

When you want to perform superbly in crucial situations—when the chips are down—you can recapture the feelings of powerful effectiveness. Fire the K-anchor, go to your place of power in actuality or in fantasy, and see the imaginary storehouse of power. Do this several hours or the night before you want to perform at your very best. Remove as *little* power as necessary by metaphorically grasping a small portion of it in your hands. Actually reach out, "grasp" power, and then bring your hands to your chest until you feel confidently energized.

PERSONAL POWER ANCHOR

1. Identify your geographical place of power.

2. Identify a past experience when you performed at your very best.

3. Anchor the physical sensations of powerful effectiveness with a natural, unobtrusive gesture (K-anchor), a special image, and a special sound or word.

4. Go to your place of power, in actuality or in fantasy; fire the K-anchor and metaphorically "deposit" the feelings of power in that place.

5. For each past and future experience of power, repeat steps 2–4 and stack the feelings of power associated with them in the same K-anchor.

6. To tap your storehouse of power when you're faced with a very important task, fire the common K-anchor, go to your place of power in actuality or in fantasy, and see the storehouse of power that you deposited there. Do this the night before or several hours before you want to perform at your very best.

7. Take as *little* power as necessary and bring it into your body until you feel confidently energized.

SIX

Just-Right State: The "Zone"

You have played almost flawlessly, with aces and other shots in all the right places. Still in a joyous sweat immediately after a round of congratulations, you have thought, perhaps aloud, "If only I could play that way all the time. It's like I was in a 'zone.'"

When a player is in the right state of mind, he can execute shot after wondrous shot throughout an entire match. When this occurs, mind, mood, and movement are solidly melded. A sense of harmony in the player's body produces rhythmical and effortless strokes; his attention is riveted on each shot, yet there is no conscious concentration. He feels as if he's in another world or in a trance—the state of being in the "zone."

This chapter focuses on the use of music, color, and images to produce effortless strokes and uncanny placement of shots.

Music and the
Tennis Player's Shots

I have noticed that athletes become transformed when music is playing in the practice arena; music seems to change the rhythm and power of their movements. I investigated how all kinds of athletes use music specifically to enhance their performance. Consequently I developed a technique—the M & M Process—to integrate music and movement. This process, described in detail a little later, consists of having athletes select music that elicits or reinforces a just-right mood or state for performing well. Their movement, mood, and the music become all of a piece. As a result they move into the "zone" and play more consistently.

Since many tennis strokes are rhythmic, and since most players have a comfortable playing tempo, it makes sense to use music to create a just-right state for both. Let's see how some tennis players have used music to enhance their game.

Using Music to
Maintain Swing Tempo

A former client of mine uses music to correct a tendency to move too quickly as he tosses the ball on his serve. When he rushes his backswing and ball toss, he loses control of his ability to vary the kind of serve he wants.

To correct this he identified several different songs that reflected his preferred serving tempo for each of his serves—flat, topspin, and kick. He listened to those songs while wearing a Walkman for several weeks during practice to get them anchored. Now, during a match, the music automatically plays in his mind and his tempo is consistently what he wants it to be.

Some players also use music to regulate the tempo for

hitting ground strokes. Terry Phelps, a WTA tour player, discovered that she always sings to herself when she's playing well; when playing poorly she gives herself negative commands that usually don't help.

After experimenting with my technique, the M & M Process, teaching pro "Tutu" Gupta now uses music regularly in her Junior Development Program. She claims that her students have a "longer and better attention span when they are receiving instruction and practicing to the sound of music."

Using Music to
Quiet the Mind

Many tennis players have developed the habit of giving themselves silent, verbal instructions before and during a point. These instructions can be okay *before* the ball is served, but there's nothing more disruptive to the unconscious regulation of the complex act of playing tennis than internal talk *during* a point. Listening to music is a marvelous way to stop your internal voices so that your unconscious mind can assume control of your game.

The M & M Process

The M & M Process is a systematic way of using music to regulate your tennis strokes. It consists of matching specific kinds of strokes with specific kinds of music. Here's how to do it.

Sitting in an armchair at home, see again in your mind a fine tennis shot, paying close attention to the feel of the rhythm and effort that characterized that shot. Then listen to different kinds of pleasing music that you think will match the stroke. Test the match between music and the action of your body and racquet. If the images of the remembered shot are clear and positive, and if you can feel your muscles contract in harmony with the music, you've got a just-right match. Then it's time to test it on the court during practice and while playing a set or two with a practice partner.

During practice, hit a dozen or so balls while listening to the selected music, using a Walkman or simply hearing a tune in your head. When you're satisfied that the music positively influences the tempo and effectiveness of your movements, anchor the music to your stroking action. While hearing the music in your mind, hit balls during daily practice or swing the racquet at home if you can't get to a court. Continue this practice for several weeks until the music becomes firmly associated with your stroking action. Eventually you'll discover that the music will automatically play in your head when you make that kind of shot.

It's important to match specific elements of music with specific parts of various shots—ground strokes, overheads, volleys, serves. The elements of music consist of pitch, harmony, tone, rhythm or beat, volume, and intensity or "energy." The parts of your tennis stroke that could be matched with the music include grip strength, tempo and length of the backswing, speed of the racquet head at impact, and follow-through.

For example, the rhythm of an entire piece of music, or even one musical phrase, might parallel your entire stroke; a syncopated rhythm might be just right to emphasize the arm action on volleys at the net; a pause or an extended note could regulate the amount of hesitation you might want just before you start your serve. The energy or loudness of one song might be appropriate for regulating the amount of effort needed to rip a passing shot down the line, while quite the opposite level of musical energy would be more suitable for stroking a delicate drop shot. A quiet ballad might be just right for a smooth, crosscourt backhand return, while Bruce Springsteen could be more fitting for an overhead forehand smash. The possibilities for "matches" between music and tennis shots are infinite.

I helped Val Paese, a nationally ranked (top 20) racquetball player, replace a harsh, critical internal voice by applying music to her game. She had a virtual rock concert automatically playing in her head during competition. For example, during her serves she heard Madonna singing "Holiday"; Madonna also sang "Get in the Groove" to her while she was hitting ceiling balls; the Pointer Sisters' "Jump" jumped onto her mental turntable when she hit hard, down-the-line kill shots; and when she felt the need to psych herself up, she heard the Pointer Sisters sing "I'm So Excited." Each of these songs matched the mood, effort, and rhythm she wanted to use while making different shots. Val used the M & M Process to create her competitive musical score.

Here are the steps to follow while using the M & M Process.

M & M PROCESS

1. Sitting somewhere comfortable at home, recall making a fine tennis shot or relive a shot you just made while practicing. See and hear what you saw and heard then and feel again the rhythm and effort of your stroke.

2. Identify several pieces of music you enjoy that you think might have the intensity, beat, rhythm, and harmony that match the entire action of your body or only an element of it.

---

3. Test the match between the music and your movement. If the images of the remembered shot are clear
and positive, if you can feel your muscles contract and
relax in harmony with the music, then it's time for
on-court encores.

4. Strap a Walkman to your waist and listen to the music
while executing that preselected shot. If you don't
have a Walkman, start the music in your mind.

5. If the shots are good, fire the musical anchor at home
and while practicing on the court for two or three
weeks or until the music plays automatically in your
head whenever you're about to make the shot on the
court.

6. Evaluate the effectiveness of the process periodically.
If the quality of the shot decreases, change the music.

Follow the same steps to identify and anchor music that
matches the just-right tempo that you find comfortable
between shots. When your opponent stalls between points,
just play your tune in your head to keep you cool. You can do
the same thing during changeovers when you're feeling
rushed or down.

Time Distortion

I'm reasonably certain you have noticed that time seems to
pass quickly or slowly depending on your mental activity. If
you've been racing around town just before going to the
court, for example, your physical state affects your mental
processing to the point that your mind is racing. In this case

you'll probably think there's not enough time to get set, and this can result in rushed and mis-hit shots.

In a different sense, if you're faced with having to make a lot of tough shots during a match, you could feel pressure to return your opponent's shots before you're ready; this, too, can result in unforced errors.

In still another sense, your body and mind might feel sluggish and tired. Shots lack crispness and your timing is slowed down. Time itself seems to slog along, with each shot taking forever to be completed.

What is needed to get your body and mind synchronized with your normal playing rhythm is a modification of your perception of time. When your perception of time changes, your sense of urgency decreases and your coordination improves. Then your game can return to its normal level of effectiveness.

While working with some figure skaters in Sun Valley several years ago, I stumbled onto two very simple procedures that affect the perception of time and the timing of coordinated movement, like spinning in figure skating, twisting in diving, and swinging a tennis racquet.

One of these techniques, the Counting Process, may remind you of the childhood game of hide-and-seek. You remember. When you were "it," you had to hide your eyes and count to 100 or some other high number. It seemed to take forever. The other, the Off-Ramp Technique, relates to the dramatic change in the sensation of speed when you leave a high-speed highway on the off ramp; then time and speed seem to slow down. One or both of these techniques will probably be useful if, for example, you want to slow down your backswing or speed up the movement of the racquet through the ball. Experiment with both techniques to discover which is best for you.

The Counting Process

This metaskills technique merely involves counting, *first very slowly, then as fast as possible*. Count silently to *10* as slowly as possible. Then count silently to *10* as quickly as possible, to *20* as quickly as possible, to *40* as quickly as possible, and finally to *50* as fast as you can. Don't skip any number, the way you might have when you played hide-and-seek. After you've finished the counting tasks, immediately hit some balls, paying attention to the tempo of your stroke. The result will probably be the exact tempo you want, whether it was too fast or too slow before you counted. This is because your perception of time has been altered and counting has distracted your conscious mind. Distracting your conscious mind lets your unconscious mind regulate the proper timing, faster or slower.

The Off-Ramp Technique

This technique consists of mentally traveling in an automobile on a superhighway at maximum speed while watching the rapidly passing, center-line markings, and seeing the light poles and trees peripherally on the side of the road. Listen to the hum of the engine and the *whoosh* of the wind as your car speeds along. Feel the vibration of the wheels through the chassis on your feet and the movement of the steering wheel in your hands.

Now imagine it's time to leave the highway as the exit ramp suddenly appears a very short distance ahead. Apply the brakes, hear the tires squeal, and feel your body being thrust forward as you quickly slow down to thirty-five, twenty-five, and fifteen miles per hour in a matter of seconds. At this point the car will seem to be crawling along to the end of the ramp.

When this mental process is complete, immediately hit a

few balls. The result will be a correction in the timing of your stroke, either a slower backswing or a faster action in the impact area of your swing, depending upon what you're working on at the moment. Again, by distracting your conscious mind from the task of tempo regulation, your unconscious mind can do its natural work unimpeded.

Color and Tennis Shots

Several years ago I had a client (I'll call her Jennifer) who frequently lost her cool after making unforced errors in competition or when a shot didn't turn out perfectly. You know the type. If the ball landed in bounds only two feet from the baseline during practice when she allowed herself only a six-inch tolerance, she'd become really angry. She would fling her racquet into the net or break it when she slammed it down into the ground. She wanted to be in control of her temper, but it got away from her more than she liked. She didn't like the fact that her anger was costing her points—to say nothing about the money she was spending on new racquets.

Together we tried a variety of techniques to get her into a just-right state or "zone" for playing up to her potential as a nationally ranked junior player. This is what worked for Jennifer. It seems that when she used self-hypnosis as a means of relaxing off the court, she always saw the color purple in her mind when she was in a deep trance state.

To make use of this relaxed state on the court, I waited for her to make an unforced error. Before she had a chance to act on her anger, I shouted, "Wait! Say to yourself, 'How can I correct that shot?' Then look up and see a purple image of yourself hitting that shot properly."

That did it. At that moment Jennifer combined what she had previously learned from self-hypnosis with a recently acquired ability to construct images of corrections instead of making repeated mental pictures of her mistakes. From that moment on, Jennifer did not throw or break any more racquets.

Jennifer practiced seeing purple images of herself making corrections after bad shots until it became automatic and eventually unconscious; the color purple became her anchor.

Jennifer's sudden change in behavior is explained in this way: First, the color purple generated a calmness within her. Second, looking upward enabled her to make clearer images; the combination of the two factors interrupted her anger.

Colored-Image Anchor

Jennifer's use of color stimulated me to develop a simpler and systematic technique for using color. It transports people into a "zone," or just-right state, for playing good tennis, and I call it the *colored-image anchor*. Here's how this anchoring process worked during one of my sessions with Matt Clark on the court.

Matt is a fine player, ranked in the top 16 in New York State doubles and number one with his partner in the state's Section 9 doubles. Even so, he normally "clutches" on his second serve whenever he is down a break or a set. His kick serves usually float over the net, landing in the middle of the service court, ready to be clobbered by his opponent. He wanted more speed and spin on the ball to make it land as far back in the box as possible.

I had him remember, as Sherlock Holmes, a time when he was serving just the way he wanted to. He recalled hitting fine kick serves in the final set at the Section 9 doubles finals in New Paltz. "Reproduce one of the best of those serves here on the practice court," I told him, "but serve as if you were back there in New Paltz."

He was able to hit several fine serves and said he felt confident serving that way.

"Repeat what you just did," I instructed him. "Only this time, as you strike the ball, still pretending you're back at New Paltz, let a color flash spontaneously into your mind's eye."

Matt served once more and said, "Blue! That's the kind of serve I want."

Then I asked him to do it again and let the blue color spontaneously become any kind of image.

Matt's image became a "blue square." I had him serve several more times while keeping the blue square in mind. He was very pleased with the results.

"In the future," I said, "especially when you get uptight, just think about the blue square and let your unconscious mind do the rest."

A day or so later Matt reported that he had had "amazing" results with his "blue square" during a three-set match. "Usually I serve about five or six double faults in each match," he told me. "But yesterday I had only one."

COLORED-IMAGE ANCHOR

1. As you hit a good shot while practicing, let a color flash into your mind when the racquet strikes the ball.

2. Repeat the shot several more times and see the color again. If they are well hit, hit another ball and let the color change spontaneously into an image when the racquet meets the ball.

> **3.** Hit the same shot several more times, again seeing the colored image in your mind; think of nothing else.
>
> **4.** Anchor this colored image a few more times daily for two or three weeks until you see it without conscious effort.
>
> **5.** If the shots are unsatisfactory, generate another colored image.

"Swish"

There's a process you can use to regain your composure after, say, losing a set when you were up 5–0. It's called "Swish" and was invented by Richard Bandler, one of the creators of NLP. The name is apt because when it works, and that's most of the time, it works quickly—swish. Its purpose is to bring about a lasting change in behavior or mood, exactly what's needed to be consistent during a match.

Recently I was working with Matt Clark at the Nevele Tennis Center in Ellenville, New York. According to his teacher, Fred Rubin, Matt had *never* smiled while playing, or even while practicing tennis—that is, until he used "Swish."

Matt concurred with Fred's observation, saying, "I have to be perfect, and I'm always upset when I'm not."

To help Matt reframe his perspective about perfection we discussed the ideas that there are no perfect performances in sports, that no performance can ever be repeated exactly, and that fine players are masters at correcting errors in their performance unconsciously in the midst of each shot (see pages 147–148).

I asked him if he thought these ideas would help him to be "looser" on the court.

"Well," he said, "it takes some of the pressure off as I think about playing average shots, but I still feel upset."

Then I asked him what might happen to his game if he were able to overcome his bad feelings about not hitting perfect shots.

"I'd probably be more relaxed on the court and have some fun. That's what my mother and Fred have been telling me for years."

"Here's what I want you to do. Remember a time when you really got frustrated, in spades, after hitting a lousy shot and losing a point, and relive that scene to the point when you're really feeling lousy again."

"There are so many," he said as he paused to think. "Oh, I've got one, a double fault. I can see a movie of both serves going into the net."

"Good," I said. "Find just one frame of that movie of those shots that represents the essence of how poorly you hit the ball and how badly you felt. Make sure it's a regular picture and project it on the palm of my hand. Let it be all one color and really feel lousy."

"Okay, it's gray," he told me as he focused on my hand. "It's a feeling of depression, a really down feeling."

Then I asked him to remember a time, unrelated to tennis since he was always a sourpuss on the court, when he felt the opposite of depression. I instructed him to find an experience when his mood was the way he normally is off the court, fun-loving and happy. He remembered a time when he was happy with a friend. I asked him to construct an internal picture of that experience, a metapicture that was really attractive—a picture that he would really like to hop into.

"What does that feel like?" I asked.

Matt's frown left his forehead; he smiled and said, "I feel relaxed and happy, no depression."

"Good. See that metapicture again and give it a color too."
He chose blue.

"Before we do the 'Swish,' I want to know what happens

inside when you let your mind go blank. Let it go blank right now."

Matt looked off into space and said, "Black. I see black."

"All right, now we can swish. Project the gray image of depression here on the palm of my hand. At the same time, see the happy blue image, about the size of a dime, superimposed on the gray image in the lower left-hand corner."

With a frown on his face Matt stared at my hand.

Continuing, I said, "What I want you to do is to *quickly* make the small, happy blue image become larger and cover the depressed gray image. Do it as fast as you can when I say 'Swish.' Ready . . . Swish!"

Matt's eyes became completely unfocused, and a smile appeared on his face. Then I asked, "What does it feel like inside after you swish?"

"I feel relaxed, happy, and lighter."

"Great. Now let's do it faster, much faster, five times in a row, letting your mind go blank in between swishes. Make sure you do them fast, the way your brain works, with your mind going to black in between."

When he had finished, I asked him to project the gray image on my hand again.

"It's hard to do," he replied.

"Good. That means it's beginning to work. During the next few weeks, practice swishing those two images four or five times a day until you're able to cover the gray image with a blue one. You can do this at home just like you did it here, and you can do it immediately after making a bad shot during tennis practice. Stop practicing the 'Swish' when it becomes automatic after a bad shot; your unconscious mind will take over."

A short while later Matt began practicing on the court with Fred, his teacher. To Fred's surprise, Matt smiled several times during the practice; the "Swish" had worked.

Here are the steps for doing the "Swish" by yourself. The

instructions that follow represent a considerably modified and simplified version of Richard Bandler's technique.

"SWISH"

1. Remember a specific time when you felt and acted in a way that interfered with playing well.

2. Identify what you saw, heard, and felt at that specific time *just before* your mood changed—netting a sitter, perhaps, that should have been a set-clinching winner. As you think about it, *make regular pictures.*

3. Select one image (a regular picture) in only one color that represents your mood and the way you acted.

4. Remember a specific experience in which your mood was *exactly opposite* of the undesired one. The experience should represent how you want to act and feel in place of the way you acted when you were in a negative mood. Watch yourself act the way you want to act *in the form of metapictures.*

5. Select one image (a metapicture) in a different color that represents the way you want to act and feel.

6. Link the two colors (from steps 3 and 5). In your mind see the first colored image—big and bright—and project it onto an imaginary screen in front of you. Then project the second colored image on top of the first color. The second color should be small and dim and located at the bottom left-hand corner of the first color.

7. Change or swish the two images *quickly* by having the small, dim one become big and bright and replace the large image.

---

8. Repeat this procedure five times, taking only one second for each repetition. Let your mind go *absolutely blank in between.*

You can test the results in several ways.

1. Project the first image onto your imaginary screen. If it's mostly covered by the second image, the "Swish" worked. If not, practice the "Swish" four or five times daily until the first image cannot be projected all by itself.

2. Project in your mind a future test situation, a shot in an important match that might result in a negative mood change. Go forward into that situation and discover whether you behave in a way you like. If the undesired mood changes to the desired one, the "Swish" worked.

3. Play a match and find out if you are able to eliminate the undesired state or at least overcome it in a matter of seconds. If you can change your mood quickly, the "Swish" has met its most difficult test.

4. If any of these tests fail, repeat the entire "Swish" process.

Free-Swing Anchor

Anchored images need not be in color, like Matt's image. Any image can represent the feeling you want when you stroke the ball, and it can be generated out of any past experience.

According to most professional tennis players, the most effective tennis strokes are the ones that feel free and effortless. Consequently, if you can create a single image that represents the idea of freedom combined with effortlessness, you will create the right amount of freedom in your mind and body to make those effortless shots that feel so great. All you need to do is to remember a time in your life, *unrelated to tennis,* when you really felt free. It might be a time when you were sunbathing on a beach, overlooking a valley from a mountaintop, or leaving school on graduation day.

While practicing, go back to that experience in your mind to feel again the bodily sensations of freedom. When you have that feeling of freedom, remember a specific scene from that time that best represents the freedom you want when you swing the racquet.

As you prepare to rally with a playing partner, project that scene of freedom onto the racquet strings and feel free in your body, especially your hands and arms. When the image is clear and you feel free in your body, move into the ready position and rally with your partner. Hit each ball, keeping that image projected onto your racquet strings throughout the entire shot.

How good was the shot? How did the stroke feel? If it was good and felt effortless, you now have a new V-anchor, an image representing freedom.

Reinforce the new anchor for several weeks whenever you practice, using all the shots in your repertoire. When you can consistently generate effortless swings, forget about consciously projecting the image onto your racquet. If your body ever gets taut when playing, consciously fire the anchor between a couple of points only; then return to playing mindlessly again.

SEVEN

The Pro Within: Your Instructional Mind

When you want to refine your tennis game, you have two experts to call on for help: a professional tennis teacher and your own mind. Both are important. You need a professionally trained teacher for help in establishing proper stroke mechanics and in developing game plans. You also need to pay attention to your internal pro, who constantly grows in experience and helps you coach yourself.

This chapter contains techniques you can use to be your own pro, to correct the mechanics of your swing, and to know the difference between how you run your brain when you're playing well and how you do when you're not. You'll also learn how to improve shots that are rusty, how to develop new shots without professional instruction, and how to establish a game plan.

Getting Good
Instruction

When you decide to secure professional help, it's absolutely essential that you choose a pro who respects and uses the power of *your* mind and can turn you back onto your own resources to improve your game. With this attitude a pro can make your learning efficient and enjoyable. The best kind of instruction not only teaches you the fundamentals of various tennis strokes but also helps you eliminate your flaws.

I encourage you to find a coach who subscribes to the learning principles of Timothy Gallwey, the author of *Inner Tennis* (W. Timothy Gallwey. *Inner Tennis: Playing the Game.* New York: Random House, 1976.) Gallwey's approach is similar although not entirely identical to mine.

I recommend that you find a coach who will help you to

- limit your attention to only important cues, one at a time
- increase your sensory awareness
- rely on your unconscious mind to regulate your game
- distract your conscious mind so that you play mindlessly
- use errors as important sources of feedback information
- stay in the here and now without dragging in the past or anticipating the future
- really know and honor what you value and want

The techniques in this chapter and others are designed to make you your own teacher yet still capable of recognizing when you need the help of a tennis pro when you get stuck.

Backup Process

Frequently advanced players are not quite sure which elements of their game to refine; nor are they sufficiently skilled in making a game plan. The Backup Process is designed to uncover unknown elements of your game that need improvement and to guide you in developing game plans against specific opponents. Essentially it consists of imagining your *anticipated* performance in a *forthcoming* match. Play the entire match in your mind, noticing your own and your opponent's winners and errors.

During your mental review defects in your performance will be revealed in the form of unclear images, garbled and discordant sounds, and uncomfortable feelings. These distorted sensory data are forms of communication from your unconscious mind about aspects of your game that need attention.

You may notice, for instance, blurred images during half volleys or crosscourt topspins; you may feel unnecessary tension in your legs as you go for half volleys; or you may hear an internal buzz as you serve. These internal A's, V's, and K's are all cues signaling that you should spend more time on those skills during practice sessions.

For instance, if you, as a left-hander, feel uncomfortable while receiving kick serves from your imaginary right-handed opponent in the deuce court, it could suggest having a practice partner serve them repeatedly so you can familiarize yourself with the spin and bounce of the ball. Or, if your pictures are fuzzy as you get ready to return an imaginary serve, it could mean that your court position and racquet preparation are defective.

Your opponent's tendencies either to play well or to make errors will also be revealed in your fantasy match. His winners and errors will provide you with internal sensory information about how you can create your game plan for the coming match. If, for example, you notice that he repeatedly blocks your hard serves to the body with high returns that you put away for winners, you will have important information for creating a plan that takes advantage of the serve-and-volley game. Or, if he frequently plays winning drop shots when he's behind, you can adjust your game plan so that you prevent him from making those shots when you're up a break.

THE BACKUP PROCESS

1. Go forward to a match against a familiar opponent. Fantasize, in full sensory detail, the entire match, noting the kinds of shots you and your opponent make.

2. See, hear, and feel all that you would expect to see, hear, and feel as you mentally play three sets. If any of the points played are incomplete, discordant, unclear, or uncomfortable during your fantasy match, it's a signal from your unconscious mind about elements of your game that need improvement.

3. After you have identified your strengths and what needs to be worked on, *take a step backward.* Fantasize how you would prepare for that competition, knowing what your mind has uncovered.

4. Repeat step 2 as you fantasize practice sessions to discover how they could be improved.

5. Get yourself a practice partner to work on what needs improvement and refine the elements of your game plan.

Repeat the Backup Process periodically to identify other weaknesses in performance. When mental rehearsals of future matches become devoid of defective sensory data, you can feel reasonably confident that you're fully prepared.

Game Plans

Many professional players rely on their personal coaches to create game plans for use against known competitors. Designing a game plan requires a lot of basic information that is not readily available to tennis players and coaches. It necessitates a sophisticated ability to identify an opponent's flaws in stroke execution.

Mike Estep, who has coached Hana Mandlikova and Martina Navratilova, is a master at detecting a player's strengths and weaknesses. He can spot a "negative" tendency in performance like a hawk. He and I spent a few hours together while he pointed out the goof tendencies of players as they were practicing. He was invariably accurate as we watched the players repeat their flaws and lose points in competition because of them. His talent is rare.

In addition to talents like Mike's, the tennis community sorely needs statistics on the performance of players for each point played in a match that can be readily notated and analyzed. These statistics would include such things as the total number of points played in the match; the number of points won and lost on the first and second services; the number of forced and unforced errors made on forehand and backhand ground strokes, overheads, and volleys; the nature of forced and unforced errors (e.g., netted, long, wide, long and wide, short and wide, topspin, slice); the number of winners made with forehand and backhand ground strokes, volleys, overheads, drop shots, topspins and slices; the number of service winners, including aces, near aces, topspin serves, flat serves, kick serves, and where the ball landed in the service court; the number of service faults, including foot faults, double faults, and serves that were netted, long, wide, and long and wide.

Many of these statistics are now being compiled by Jon Gibbs of TenniSTAT in New Jersey. Jon is presently collecting these kinds of statistics for grand slam events and is developing a computer software program that may reveal the various points during a match and the various types of shots that are mentally troublesome for particular players.

Armed with this kind of information, players can examine the statistics pertaining to their own competitive performance as another way to identify the parts of their game that need practice. And they can examine their own statistics and those of their opponents and themselves as additional ways to develop game plans.

The Difference That Makes the Difference

Many players are habitually inconsistent when playing certain kinds of shots, and they can't figure out why. I have found that the way the player processes very small bits of information—visual, auditory, and kinesthetic—determines whether he will play a particular shot well. Your pro within can identify the differences in these bits of information between a good and a not-so-good shot.

One afternoon I was working with Ellen Beaumel, who invariably felt quite nervous at the start of most of her matches against equal or superior players. As a result of her nervousness she frequently played at a performance level far below her ability. She believed that if she could always be in a better mood at the beginning of each match she'd become more successful.

This is how I instructed Ellen to learn how to control her emotional state against a formidable opponent. The technique I taught her is called *Discovering Difference*. Its essence is to discover the difference in the way the brain works while regulating good and bad states as well as regulating good and bad shots.

I asked Ellen to remember playing a specific point when she felt confident during a tough match and to relive it as Sherlock Holmes, seeing, hearing, and feeling what she had seen, heard, and felt then. I also had her relive a specific point played during a match when she had been exceptionally nervous.

I said to Ellen, "File away in your memory for a minute or two the internal and external A's and V's and K's that were operating during both of those experiences." I emphasized that I wanted her to identify the submodality differences, that is, to notice, for example, differences in visual focus, sound volume, and muscular tension.

Ellen closed her eyes and recaptured the memories of the two experiences and said, "Okay."

"Now we're going to find out the difference that makes the difference between those two experiences," I said. "As you think about the submodalities of the A's and V's and K's for each of those experiences, what was different about them? Let's consider the difference in V's first.

"The main visual difference," she answered, "was that I had a very tight, close-up focus on my opponent when I was confident. When I was nervous, I had wide-angle focus; my opponent appeared to be a long way off."

"And the auditory differences?" I asked.

"When I felt strong, I could distinctly hear the ball when it struck our racquets; when I was nervous, I heard nothing."

"And the differences in the feeling?"

"Oh, that's the easiest to remember," she replied. "I felt springy tension in my legs and strength in my arms and shoulders when I was playing well. My stomach was like a knot when I was in my anxious state."

"Of all those differences, which one do you think would make the most difference in how you played?" I asked.

"I'm not really sure, but I think it's the focus. If I keep a tight focus on my opponent," she replied, "I think I'll feel in command of myself."

Then I had Ellen think about a tough match coming up soon, first playing that match in her mind while deliberately maintaining a wide-angle focus and then playing it with a tight focus. She did this and said that she felt good throughout the entire fantasy match when she was highly focused and very nervous when she used wide-angle imagery.

I suggested that she maintain a tight focus during her practice sessions and fantasize the forthcoming match with a tight focus every day. She reported that she followed my recommendations and played well during the actual match, keeping her eyes tightly focused on her opponent throughout. Now, when she feels queasy about a match, she regularly employs a tight visual focus to stabilize herself. The difference that made the difference in her performance was simply paying attention to the visual submodality of focus.

While working with other tennis players I have found a number of unique differences that make the difference. One player was extremely aware of silently telling himself how and where to serve. He discovered that the difference between good and bad serves was the tone of his internal voice. On good serves his voice was calm; on bad ones he said he sounded like a marine sergeant shouting drill commands.

Another player, Sheila Peck, said she was able to hit her ground strokes with much more power when she "heard" the ball scream like a banshee on contact; when she hit weak shots, she "heard" nothing in her mind. Now she regularly calls up the wail of the banshee whenever she wants to put lots of "pace" on the ball.

Here are the instructions for determining the difference that makes the difference for you.

DISCOVERING DIFFERENCE

1. Identify two similar rallies or shots, one that was excellent and one that was terrible.

2. Relive each point or shot separately, making notes of the auditory, visual, and kinesthetic submodality representations that were involved in the two experiences.

3. Compare those submodality representations to determine the differences in nature, *not in content*. For example, pictures might vary in focus or brightness, sounds might vary in volume or tone, and feelings might vary in intensity or location in the body. (See Appendix B for additional ways to vary the A's, V's, and K's.)

4. Select one difference and apply it to making a shot while practicing. Use the difference you found for the bad shot first, then for the good shot. Repeat this five or six times.

5. Evaluate the shots. If there is no difference, repeat to make sure.

6. If there's a difference, adjust your internal visual and auditory processing to include the difference when you are not playing well.

Developing New Shots

After you've developed the fundamentals of serving, ground strokes, and net play, it's natural to want to learn new shots that require skills beyond the beginner level—shots requiring topspin and underspin, overheads, half volleys, and the like. In addition, for those who have had to lay off tennis for a season or two, it's important to get back some of the skills that inevitably were "lost" in the interim.

I've developed two metaskills techniques to help you refine your skills by yourself—the Get-It Process and the Get-It-Back Process. These have proven to be very useful, not only to tennis players but to athletes in many different sports.

The Get-It Process

You may remember the fellow I introduced at the beginning of the book, Michael Gratz, the junior tennis player who wanted to hit backhand overheads like Billie Jean King. Here's how Michael used the Get-It Process with me several years ago to develop that shot. Michael is presently the number one singles player for the Brandeis University team.

During one of our sessions together I started the process by asking Michael when he had last seen Billie Jean hit a backhand overhead. He indicated that he had watched her hit a marvelous winner at Madison Square Garden a week or so earlier. So I had him project a movie of Billie Jean making that past overhead winner on the back of my left hand. I said this was his "criterion" or model that I wanted him to reproduce.

Michael focused on the back of my hand, moved his racquet slightly, nodded, looked up, and said, "Okay."

"Now, what I want you to do is to change the movie of Billie Jean to become you, Michael. See yourself in the clothing you have on now, making that shot, and feel your muscles working as you watch yourself stroke the ball."

Michael nodded as he continued to focus on my hand. Then I said, "Change the image from watching yourself from the outside to seeing what you would be seeing if you were right there in the Garden making the shot. Change from a metamovie to a regular movie and see only what you would normally see while backing up and then hitting the overhead. And really feel the shot throughout your entire body."

After a few seconds I asked, "What happened in your mind as you did that?"

"I made the shot; it went in," he answered.

Michael and I were working together at an indoor court in Riverdale, New York. We had a ball machine that made it easy for me to use the Get-It Process.

"Okay," I said. "I'll start the machine, and you reproduce the overhead five or six times."

After hitting several shots I called Michael over to the sideline and asked him to project onto my right palm a meta-movie of the best of the shots he had just hit. Then I had him compare that movie to the criterion movie of Billie Jean on the back of my left hand. I asked, "As you compare the two, what one, *and only one,* thing in your best shot do you want to correct so that it comes as close to looking like Billie Jean's as possible?"

Michael glanced back and forth between my two hands and

said, "I want to reach higher, with my arm straight, as I hit the ball."

"Do that now, without striking a ball," I said. "And as you do it, let a metaphorical image flash into your mind right at the top of the swing."

Michael swung his racquet several times and said, "I see a narrow pole become strapped to my arm at the very top of the swing to keep it straight."

"Fine. This time test that image in your mind without swinging the racquet. See if it works in your head."

Michael tested it that way and then hit a few balls. "How did it go?" I asked as he came over to the sideline.

"It's still not right," he replied. "My arm is straight at the top, but I want more wrist flexion when I strike the ball. Now the ball is going much too deep."

"Make another metamovie of yourself as you hit the ball with more wrist flexion and project it here on my right hand; compare it to your ideal overhead on my left hand."

Michael looked at my two hands and said, "That's the correction I want. It matches Billie Jean's shot."

"Can you think of another metaphorical image related to the pole strapped to your outstretched arm that would represent the wrist action?"

Michael thought for a moment and said, "Yeah, it reminds me of flicking a fly with a flyswatter."

"Now," I said, "as you see that metaphorical image in your mind as you swing your racquet, find out if it gets you what you want."

"Not quite," he answered. "I need a close target." Then, after a pause, he smiled and said, "I know. I'll pretend that I have another pole sticking out behind me at shoulder level and at right angles to the first pole with a small basket attached to the end of it. I can flick the fly right into the basket."

I laughed and told him to "chunk" the three images—the pole on the straight arm, the flyswatter, and the basket on the end of the other pole—so they would combine into *one* metaphorical image.

Laughing, Michael said, "I see a fly being swatted and dropping right into the basket. I'm pretty sure it'll work on the court."

Michael returned to hitting balls while making the new, chunked image of flicking a fly in his mind; almost every ball landed crosscourt close to the net and the sidelines. He grinned from ear to ear and said, "That's it. That's perfect."

At about that time Michael's coach came out of his office. Michael and I were both astounded to hear him say, "Hey, Michael. When did you learn Billie Jean's backhand overhead?"

To make sure that Michael's overheads continued to work I had him consciously anchor them with the fly-flicking image three or four times a day for several weeks until the image flashed into his mind automatically. Recently, five years later, he told me that he still executes that shot well. He says it's one of his strongest "weapons."

THE GET-IT PROCESS

This technique is based on the element of mimicry and the fundamental process of constantly making mental comparisons between what you're actually doing and what you want to do ideally.

1. During practice, identify a time when you observed a fine tennis player execute a shot you want to learn.

2. On an imaginary screen, flash a movie of that player making that intriguing shot.

3. Put yourself into that movie, wearing the clothing you have on now, and feel the movements involved in executing that shot.

4. Change that metamovie into a regular movie and feel the movements of making the shot.

5. Immediately hit several balls without further preparation. If you "get it," repeat it several times a day for several weeks, until it becomes automatic.

6. If you don't "get it," and most don't the first time, make a metamovie of your last attempt and compare it to the original criterion movie in step 2. Identify by feel the muscle and joint actions needed to make the correction.

7. Execute the shot several more times while paying attention *only* to the one desired correction from step 6. If the shots are satisfactory, you're finished. Practice for the next few weeks until it becomes automatic.

8. Many players don't "get it" even after a second try. In that case, go back and make another meta movie of your last shot and compare it again to the step-2 original. Ask yourself what *one* correction should be made. Identify the feelings necessary to make the additional correction.

In your mind, visualize the shot by "chunking" the two corrections (steps 6 and 8). Chunking facilitates concentration on only one correction.

Execute the shot several times more, paying attention *only* to the chunked correction. If that works, *you really are finished.*

USING METAPHORS

Metaphors can be created to anchor the result of the Get-It Process. Here's how to create a metaphorical anchor.

1. When you identify a correction, create a metaphorical representation of it. (Michael created an image of a pole strapped to his arm.)

2. Execute the shot several times while paying attention *only* to the metaphor. If the shot is satisfactory, the metaphor becomes the anchor.

3. If the first correction is made, but the shot is still unsatisfactory, visually compare it to the criterion and identify another correction. Make a metaphorical representation of this second correction. (Michael chose swatting a fly into a basket.)

4. Visualize making the shot by "chunking" the two corrections into one metaphor. If the shot is satisfactory, the chunked metaphor becomes the anchor.

Although it is helpful to create metaphors when correcting tennis strokes, it's not absolutely necessary. Whether you make metaphors or not depends on the ease with which you generate them and the degree to which they facilitate or hinder your progress. For these reasons you can be flexible in the way you approach the use of metaphorical images.

The function of a metaphor is to quiet your conscious mind so your unconscious mind can do its work without interruption. All of the neuromuscular action that is necessary for hitting the ball well is unconsciously associated with the metaphor.

Get-It-Back Process

The steps of the Get-It-Back Process are the same as for the Get-It Process. The only difference between the two is the person in the first movie (step 2). Instead of the player being Graf or Lendl, it's you. It's you executing a shot in the past that you want to get back.

I worked with Michael Gratz recently, and he told me that he wanted to get more power into his serves. I asked him to recall a specific effective serve he had made in the past. As he relived that serve in his mind, he realized that he wanted to slow down the initial movements of his backswing and ball toss.

I told Michael to hit a few serves with those slower movements and to judge only the power of his serve; no judgment was to be applied to where the serve landed. I had him rate the amount of power generated on a scale of one to five. His rating on these serves was only three.

After comparing a mental movie of one of the better serves with a mental movie of his ideal serve, he identified his legs and lower torso as the source of his power and decided to emphasize the movements of those parts of his body during the next round of what I called "curiosity serves." I encouraged him to continue being curious, scanning his body from head to toe for feelings of power.

Michael hit another dozen balls and rated most of them as fours. He again compared the best of these serves with his ideal serve. He discovered that he wanted to create a flow of power that began in his legs and midsection and to gradually release that power through his racquet.

I asked him if there was a metaphor that he could use to

represent that gradual release of power. He thought of a large, foamy blue wave, gradually curling and spilling onto a beach.

This metaphor turned out to be exactly what he wanted. He began to serve with one powerful wavelike action time after time as he thought about the ocean wave breaking on the beach. He rated these serves as four-and-a-half. I reminded him to consciously use the wave image until it became automatic. This process would allow his unconscious mind to take over his serves.

Holographic Viewing

Holographic viewing is a systematic process of imagery that registers a proper swing pattern in your neuromuscular system, in the brain-nerve-muscle connections that make a tennis shot happen. It consists of watching a good player from different positions "around the clock." That is, watch him or her on the court from the front, back, sides, and positions in between, as long as you can keep out of the way of play.

Holographic viewing is quite precise. Immediately after you watch a player hit, close your eyes and make an internal movie that reproduces the shot. Consciously feel your muscles become active while looking at the movie. When you're reasonably certain your internal movie accurately reproduces the player's swing, move to a different position and watch him swing again. Make another internal movie and feel the swing in your muscles as before. Repeat this process until you have viewed your model tennis player hit the same shot from various positions "around the clock."

Now you have a set of criterion movies of a swing that you want to match in the Get-It Process described earlier. Not only do you have a model to copy, but you have already put into your brain much of the neural activity you need to reproduce the desired shot. Many people have told me that by just passively observing tennis matches live or on TV for several hours on a weekend, their games improve during the next week.

The imagery techniques described in this chapter can be used for any kind of shot; they will be particularly useful in developing new ones. Putting yourself into Boris Becker's place as he's playing at the net or into Steffi Graf's as she hits backhand slices may not put you on the pro tour, but it's worth the effort to improve your game.

Paradoxical Intention

A master's tennis competitor—I'll call him Jonathan—came to me for help in making his game more consistent. As we explored what happened in his mind when he played badly, he said, "Every time my game goes downhill I see an image of my father seated in the gallery scowling at me. That image really bugs me because it won't go away."

This is what I told him to do: "During all of your practice sessions and informal matches, imagine being observed by a large gallery of spectators; and I want all of the spectators in the gallery to be your scowling father watching you every time you hit either a really fine shot or a poor one."

Jonathan did this for several weeks and learned that he could control the image of his father, making it appear and disappear when he wanted it to. Now that he was no longer the victim of an uncontrollable image, that image of his father eventually lost its negative power.

This unusual process is called *paradoxical intention.* It is one way to get rid of an unwanted and seemingly uncontrollable behavior. By deliberately exaggerating his father's image on good *and* bad shots, Jonathan learned how to regulate his emotional response to it and regained his confidence. The paradox is intentionally using a behavior that caused a problem to get rid of the problem.

EIGHT

Self-Hypnosis: Tapping the Power of Your Unconscious Mind

Athletes in all sports have told me that their best performances occur in states that are absolutely mindless. Without any thought whatsoever they know that a shot will be good *before* they hit it. I'm sure that has also happened to you.

These high-performance states are essentially trances that make it possible for the unconscious mind to control performance without interference from the conscious mind. The characteristics of high-performance states in tennis vary from person to person. Some have been described as "lightness of body," "flowing rhythm," "vibrating energy," and "perfect wholeness."

Other descriptions of these altered states include "The ball got bigger and brighter"; "My hand and racquet seemed to be all one unit"; "One small part of my opponent's court lit up, and my ball just went there without my directing it"; "It was like I was in a soundproofed bubble"; and "Time slowed down so much that I seemed to have forever to make a shot."

In contrast to these positive trance states there are many players who generate negative trance states through intense self-criticism. They are constantly in a depressed state. I'm sure you've played with people like this. They're the ones who are always talking to themselves, silently and out loud. They are telling themselves what not to do and chastising themselves by saying things like "Why did you flub that shot?" and "You jerk, your game stinks," and "You can't play worth. . . ." Essentially they generate unconscious, negative imagery and muscle feelings and form a negative perception of themselves that often becomes a self-fulfilling prophecy. And they usually feel rushed, never having enough time to plan their shots or to follow their game plan. Needless to say, their performance is erratic and shots go all over the lot when they're in that state.

Time and the Unconscious Mind

When I reflect on what athletes have told me about good and bad performance states, one characteristic seems to stand out: the sense that time slows down. They are astounded by the extremely slow movement of their opponents, themselves, and the ball. They seem to have all the time in the world to prepare for a shot because their opponents seem to "telegraph" their next move far in advance.

When this phenomenon occurs, the athlete is in a deep trance state and experiences the pure working of the unconscious mind. That work, unconscious information processing, is unbelievably precise and rapid. In a flash it absorbs and integrates all the minute, yet critically important, cues in the environment that are needed to perform well; none of this information is in the athlete's conscious awareness.

When, in a trance state, the athlete experiences this

enormous amount of mental activity, the only way he or she can process it is to slow time down. Of course time continues on its way, second by second, but it is perceived as changed since the athlete's state is changed. Moreover, since the athlete's conscious mind is quiet and inactive, it becomes an observer of this exquisite regulator of behavior, the unconscious mind.

All of this suggests that if superb performance is the desired outcome, then athletes need to learn how to perform without conscious attention so that the unconscious mind can do its job without interruption. Learning how to perform in a trance state, then, is essential.

Many of the metaskills techniques in this book generate mild trance states. Now I want you to learn how to induce profound trance states in yourself so that you can play even better.

The Nature of Trance

Many people have a mistaken notion about trance, believing that it's a mystical phenomenon, attainable only by some people. It's not. Contrary to the opinion of some hypnosis specialists, anyone can learn how to get into a trance. Those who assert that some people cannot be hypnotized are mistaken. The late Dr. Milton H. Erickson, a renowned medical hypnotherapist whose work served as one foundation stone of Neuro-Linguistic Programming, was one of the first to recognize the naturalness of trance, and he incorporated it into his remarkably unique and successful practice.

All people have the ability to induce a trance state in themselves; that is, they can change their state of consciousness. It's just a matter of taking time to redevelop the appropriate mental processes to do so. Like children, we have the innate capacity to become instantly enraptured by the simplest experience, but overemphasis on rationality by our educational system has dampened our respect for the unconscious.

Children naturally become deeply engrossed in the simple pleasures of watching birds or kites soar in the sky, of listening to buzzing bees as they hover over flowers to extract their nectar, of losing track of time and space before the television screen. They become transported from the here and now into their world of fantasy and right-brain mental activity.

Adults too know what it's like to alter their states of consciousness, but frequently they forget they know. Like children, they're awed by sunsets, transformed by music, enchanted by novels and stories, absorbed in thought while waiting for a traffic light to change, and their moods are altered by hundreds of everyday experiences in a matter of seconds. Trances are induced by riding in elevators, driving long distances on interstate highways, listening to the clickety-clack of the wheels on railroad tracks, making love, focusing intensely on a tennis ball, and recalling the details of a superb past tennis shot as if they were Sherlock Holmes.

Putting Hypnosis to Work

Having studied and experimented with hypnosis in athletics, I'm convinced that it's perhaps the most powerful tool athletes can use to regulate the consistency of their performance. Essentially hypnosis is a process of creating, intensifying, and stabilizing an inner-directed state of consciousness. Most of my metaskills techniques are based on this process and are designed to tap the resources of the unconscious mind by distracting and quieting the conscious mind.

The Sherlock Holmes Exercise in Chapter 2 induces and stabilizes the hypnotic phenomenon of age regression—going back to a former time and place in your life. The M & M Process, anchoring colors, and various forms of imagery discussed in preceding chapters also stimulate hypnotic processes. Metaphors in particular, like story telling, generate states most conducive to fine athletic performance. Metaskills techniques activate the nondominant hemisphere of the brain, precisely the part of the brain that is fully activated during trance. These trance states open the door for expanding our world of inner experiences that are essential to making changes in outward behavior. They can free the tennis player's imagination while implementing a game plan.

Several athletes with whom I have worked have experimented with performing *simple, safe skills* after hypnotizing themselves. They invariably report that their performance becomes almost effortless. Figure skaters have traced their figures in competition while in a trance; a golfer has developed a way to play golf while deliberately going into trance just before hitting each shot, returning to a normal state in between shots; and a distance swimmer "goes off" into his own world of music while swimming 400-meter and 1,500-meter races.

Self-Hypnosis

For you to hypnotize yourself requires a certain mind-set to begin with. Essentially you let yourself go and give yourself permission to experience your inner world fully, gradually becoming less and less aware of external reality, like Zen meditation. Just let your mind go in a consciously suggested direction, yet allow it to generate whatever sensory representations it wants to with absolutely no conscious control.

This means letting go of ordinary ways of thinking, adopting an attitude of curiosity and a desire to learn from the hypnotic experience.

I have taught hundreds of athletes a simple form of self-hypnosis. *After it is learned,* you can use it to tap internal resources and achieve important outcomes. The technique was developed by Betty Erickson, Dr. Milton Erickson's wife. I have modified it slightly. It's really quite simple.

Read over the instructions below and the descriptions of the reactions of people who have experienced the technique. This will answer some of your questions about what to expect from being in an altered state. Later, when you feel comfortable about hypnotizing yourself, memorize the steps in the process, follow them, and go into an altered state.

The Betty Erickson Technique (Modified)

Sit comfortably in a quiet place where you won't be disturbed. Separate your legs slightly and rest your forearms and hands comfortably on your thighs. Support your head by resting it against the back of a chair or against the wall.

Step 1. Metapicture
With your eyes open or closed, make a metapicture of yourself seated as you are. When you have a clear metapicture of yourself, gently close your eyes and hold that picture for a few seconds.

Step 2. See, Hear, and Feel
Now, *with your eyes closed, see* pictures in your mind of any *three* objects in the room; *hear* any *three* sounds in the surrounding environment, such as a ticking clock or traffic noises outside; and *feel* any *three* things on the surface of your body. Then see any *two* things, hear any *two* sounds, and feel

any *two* physical sensations as before. And then see *one* thing, hear *one* thing, and feel *one* thing.

Step 3. Go to a Place of Pleasure

Now become aware of one hand and arm getting heavier than the other. You can press that hand down against your thigh. The lighter arm may begin to bend, and your hand may lift upward. The movement will be ever so slow, jerky, and automatic. In your mind, go to a place of pleasure, a place where you've been before and where you have thoroughly enjoyed yourself. See, hear, and feel again what you saw, heard, and felt before in that special place of yours. Enjoy again the experiences you had there.

At some time during this recollection of pleasure you'll begin to notice that the rate and depth of your breathing have changed, your heart rate has changed, and your sense of the weight of your arms and legs has changed. You might also notice that one of your hands has lifted. When you notice any of these changes, use them as a signal for you to let your mind go wherever it wants to go, becoming passively curious about what will happen next in your mind.

Step 4. Back to "Normal"

At some point your unconscious mind will give you a signal—in the form of a personally meaningful image, sound, or bodily sensation—that implies it is time to begin to return to your original normal state. For instance, if your hand rose during the process, its slow movement downward is a signal to return to normal.

Rouse yourself gradually by opening your eyes, looking at the objects around you, listening to the sounds in the environment, and moving parts of your body. Be sure that you are fully alert before you engage in an activity that could result in injury.

Reactions to
Self-Hypnosis

I've taught this form of self-hypnosis to many groups of athletes. The following is an account of the reactions of one group immediately after they had experienced an altered state using the Betty Erickson Technique. At the end of the session the group gradually returned to the here and now. It took about two or three minutes for all to reorient themselves.

"I'm curious to know what reactions, questions, and comments you have about your hypnotic experience," I told the group when they all appeared to be alert.

Kathryn initiated the response: "I felt as if I'd been asleep, but I know I was listening to your voice and following your suggestions."

Another reaction came from Bruce: "It was different for me. Once my arm started to lift, I just tuned you out altogether. I was in my own world."

In contrast Maria said, "I was so surprised when my arm started to lift. I kept peeking at it, wondering if there was something wrong with me, because it didn't go up at first. But I finally ignored it, and then it started up all by itself."

"I was really disappointed when my arm didn't come up," Gordon commented. "When you said that I didn't have to listen to your voice, I noticed that I got very warm and my arms and legs felt very heavy. It was a pleasant, relaxed feeling. That was certainly a different state from when I started the exercise."

Peter reported his experience by saying, "I sure was surprised when I didn't experience the deep relaxation that I've heard should happen during hypnosis. Instead I felt quite excited."

"My guess," I told him, "is that you were reexperiencing an exciting event in that special place of pleasure."

"That's right," he agreed. "I was riding a huge wave in the surf at the seashore."

Then I asked if any of them had *not* gone into an altered state.

"I didn't," Cheryl answered. "I tried to get relaxed, but it just didn't work."

"That's okay," I said. "This technique might not be the best way for you. Perhaps you didn't follow the instructions. You said that you '*tried* to relax.' That's a difficult thing to do. Trying to relax is like trying to be spontaneous or trying to go to sleep. Those three states—relaxation, spontaneity, and sleep—just happen; they can't be engineered."

If you have an experience similar to Cheryl's, I suggest that you do the exercise several more times. If you're still unsuccessful, it doesn't mean you are unhypnotizable. It merely means that another form of hypnosis, tailored to your individual way of processing sensory information, is necessary. Deciding the most useful form, however, requires some individual attention by a qualified clinician.

Loren had looked uncomfortable during the hypnosis session, opening her eyes several times during the exercise. "If you're willing to talk about it," I said, "would you tell us about your experience?"

"I didn't want to do it at all," she replied. "Frankly, I was afraid. I didn't want to lose control."

"I'm glad you chose not to," I responded. "When you have more trust in me, perhaps you'll be willing to experience it.

"To learn this technique requires that you give up a certain amount of control by your conscious mind and let yourself go, the way I want you to hit a tennis ball—mindlessly. It means that you will trust the process and your unconscious mind to take care of you as it has throughout your life.

"Whether you realize it or not, your unconscious mind has been taking care of you all along. For example, with your conscious mind you make a decision to hit a deep, crosscourt forehand. As you're stroking the ball, your unconscious mind controls and coordinates all the muscles in your body as you stroke the ball; things are going too fast for your conscious mind to tell individual muscles when to contract and release. Take tying your shoes as another example. You learn to tie them consciously, and now you probably tie them unconsciously, without thinking. I'm sure you trust yourself to tie your shoes without thinking, don't you?"

"Yes, but that's different," Loren answered. "I'm afraid of losing control. When I tie my shoes, I'm still able to decide what to do; I'm in control. But in hypnosis I might not be able to control anything."

At that point another member of the group with whom I had worked previously turned to Loren and said, "I think I know what you're saying. The first time Mac worked with me I was scared too. But we agreed on a signal—blinking my eyes—that I would use if things became uncomfortable. When I knew that I could stop the process, I felt in control. But I had to be willing to give up some conscious control, which was scary at first."

"You see," I said to the group, "it *is* important to be wary if you're overly susceptible to the suggestions and influence of other people, because hypnosis can be used manipulatively. However, I'm teaching you a process that you'll use by yourself. It requires that you have trust in yourself. The most important point I want to make about self-hypnosis is that eventually you'll be able to tap the power of your unconscious mind and make changes in your behavior."

The last question in the group session came from Loren. "Can you get stuck in an altered state," she asked, "and not be aware of danger, a fire, or an intruder?"

"My personal experience with self-hypnosis," I replied, "and the reported experiences of hundreds of others with whom I've worked, is that the unconscious mind is constantly and protectively monitoring the environment while you're in an altered state. When something very unusual occurs, you will be roused from the trance state. As for getting stuck, I don't know anyone who stayed hypnotized longer than the time they set aside for it. It's possible, however, that you could fall asleep if your body needs rest. When that happens, the hypnotic state is erased."

Experiencing Self-Hypnosis

If, after reading about the reactions to the Betty Erickson Technique, you feel comfortable and can see yourself doing it, then go back to page 114 and reread the steps in the process. Memorize them and go to a quiet place, where you won't be disturbed, to experience the technique.

I encourage you to practice it every few days for several weeks until you can put yourself into an altered state within a few minutes. Each time you use it, decide on the amount of time you want to remain in an altered state so you can return to your normal activities when you want to. Your unconscious mind has its own timer, and I think you'll be surprised to find that you'll "come back" within a minute or two of the time you have established for yourself.

It's important to carefully monitor your state of consciousness *after* you return to the here and now. Determine exactly how long it takes you to return completely to your normal state of functioning. Most people come back to "normal" in a matter of moments; a few take up to an hour. It's possible to injure yourself if you engage in a potentially harmful activity before you're back to your normal state.

Applying Self-Hypnosis

Self-hypnosis can be used in many ways to achieve worth-while outcomes pertaining directly to tennis or your general well-being. I mentioned a few earlier. Here are some specific ways that people have applied self-hypnosis.

For General Well-Being and Health

An older, active, recreational athlete I knew used self-hypnosis to stop smoking cigarettes after smoking a pack a day for almost 40 years. Smoking was interfering with his breathing when he played squash, and he knew it wasn't healthful.

Just before using self-hypnosis he instructed his unconscious mind to activate all the resources within himself that would make his heart and lungs function effectively and to make his lungs clean and healthy. He also told his unconscious mind to do its work in its own way, in its own time. He followed the steps of the Betty Erickson Technique, remaining in an altered state for about 20 minutes.

He told me he didn't recall noticing any special images, memories, or sounds during that altered state. It was deep and relaxed. Nothing happened for about three weeks, and he continued to smoke. So he repeated the process.

A week or so later he woke up with a bad head cold. Because he didn't get much pleasure from smoking when he had a cold, his unconscious mind apparently chose that time to go to work. After several days of suffering from a miserable cold, he realized that he hadn't smoked for two days. He didn't stop deliberately; he just didn't smoke and wasn't aware that he had stopped, because he had no withdrawal symptoms. Almost 10 years later he still doesn't smoke.

Several years ago I worked with an athlete who was an

insomniac. She wanted to sleep six hours a night instead of her usual two or three. While in bed before going to sleep, Sandy always reviewed in her mind what she wanted to do the next day. She'd worry so much about what had to be done the next day that she couldn't get to sleep.

During self-hypnosis an image of a piece of paper containing a list of chores flashed into her mind. From that image she decided to make a list *before* she went to bed of all the things she wanted to do the next day. By making the list *before* bedtime, she was more relaxed and overcame her insomnia.

Improving Athletic Skills

I also recall a high-jumper who wasn't jumping as well as he had been. He experimented with modifying several parts of his performance, but without success. He decided to try self-hypnosis, instructing his unconscious mind to attend to the task of improving his jumping. During one session he had the image of a space shuttle blasting off from Cape Canaveral. He interpreted this image to mean he should apply more energy during his takeoff. It was obvious, yet he hadn't thought of it during his experiments. So at his next practice session he created that metaphorical image of the space shuttle at the time of takeoff, and he soared over the bar with an inch or two to spare.

There are several ways to improve your tennis through self-hypnosis. One is to give yourself the suggestion beforehand to experience fully a particular problem you are having with a certain kind of shot, followed by an experience that is exactly the opposite—when you were hitting that shot well. Then put yourself into an altered state and learn how to correct your preparation and swing from the images that are unconsciously produced. After "coming back" from the altered state, compare the images of the good and bad shots, looking for ways to correct your swing. It is similar to using the Get-It-Back Process and Discovering Difference.

Using Television

Another way to use self-hypnosis consists of watching video-tape recordings of either yourself or professional players making a good shot, *after* you've put yourself into an altered state.

Many tennis shops have videotapes of fine players for sale or rent at reasonable rates. Pros also make video recordings of their students for a nominal fee. It's also possible to have continuous replays of one or more shots reproduced on one videotape. The cost varies from one area of the country to another, but it can be done in a week's time for under $100.

Here are the steps to follow if you want to view videotapes of yourself or other tennis players while in an altered state. The idea is to refine and groove your preparation and stroke for a variety of shots.

VIDEO OBSERVATION

1. Select the videotape of a top professional or yourself making a shot you want to mimic.

2. Give yourself the general suggestion to focus only on the central elements of the shot you're about to observe.

3. Put yourself into an altered state. When you're ready, turn on the VCR, but keep the sound off. While you're

---

watching, put yourself into the picture and feel the mechanics of the preparation and racquet action in your muscles.

4. When you're finished, allow yourself to come back to your "normal" state.

5. If it's convenient, go to a court to reproduce the video images as closely as possible. You may use the Get-It Process or the Get-It-Back Process, whichever is appropriate.

Here is a summary of the steps to follow in using self-hypnosis to improve your game.

ACHIEVING OUTCOMES WITH SELF-HYPNOSIS

1. Carefully specify what you want to accomplish.

2. Ask your unconscious mind to uncover all of the appropriate abilities and emotional states that will be needed to achieve the desired outcome and to apply them when it's most appropriate.

3. Put yourself into an altered state, being curious about whether or not your unconscious mind will communicate in the form of spontaneous images, sounds, and feelings. Note what happens and analyze the meaning of these events *after* you come out of the altered state.

4. Interpret any images, sounds, and feelings as being *possible* ways to achieve your outcome. Put those ways into action and evaluate their effectiveness.

5. If you have no direct communication in the form of sights, sounds, and feelings from your unconscious mind during the altered state, do nothing deliberately to achieve your desired outcome. Trust your unconscious mind to do its work. Wait for several weeks. If you still haven't achieved your desired outcome, repeat the entire process.

NINE

Mind and Body: Generating Energy, Controlling Pain, and Hastening Healing

Long five-set matches in the boiling sun can drain your energy to the point where you cannot play your very best. Painful tennis elbows, strained backs, groin pulls, and torn knee ligaments also reduce your effectiveness on the court and they take the fun out of the game. When fatigue or painful injuries interfere with your game, several techniques can help you get back into full action as quickly as possible.

These techniques for generating energy, controlling pain, and hastening healing are based on the principle that the mind affects the internal working of all the organs and systems of the body. Although we have very few hard scientific data that verify this principle, many physicians and other health specialists support it.

I know from my clinical experience, as do other medical and mental health specialists, that the mind is a fantastic energizer. I know it acts like a powerful anesthetic, and it heals without chemical supplements or scalpels.

It is evident in the experience of those who undergo chest and abdominal surgery with self-hypnosis and *without* anesthesia; it is clear through the work of faith healers, shamans, and Native American medicine men; and it has been demonstrated by hundreds of people who cure themselves of all sorts of diseases.

All I ask is that you experience doing the techniques. Find out what happens when you use them. The absolute worst that can happen, if they work, is that you'll no longer have excuses for not playing well.

Before you use these techniques, however, **I encourage you to consult your physician if you are run-down and out of shape, have unexplained pain or other physical symptoms, or are emotionally upset.** My techniques are meant to complement the work of health specialists, not to replace their services.

Energy Regulation

The spirit and physical capacity of the human being to accomplish extraordinary tasks in the face of utter fatigue are amazing. War veterans know only too well the meaning of carrying on with little or no sleep for days on end. As a coach I observed firsthand almost unbelievable performances by my swimmers during grueling practice sessions. Similarly, during the 1989 French Open, Michael Chang summoned energy from who knows where to offset his excruciating leg cramps and defeat Ivan Lendl.

I know we can tap into our past memories of having overcome fatigue as a way to deal with present tiredness. Consequently I developed one simple anchoring technique that has proved to be effective in overcoming fatigue and maintaining a high-energy state for a short period of time.

Energy Anchor

The essence of the energy anchor is to remember a time when you overcame intense fatigue in the past—seeing, hearing, and feeling again, in specific detail, what you saw, heard, and felt then. Consider the following kinds of past experiences: (1) After a tedious day at work, you engaged in an enjoyable physical activity and then felt renewed. (2) After a hard stint of labor that left you exhausted, you realized that with one last big push you could finish the task at hand; and when you finished, you felt a sense of relief, satisfaction, and restored vigor. (3) By taking a break from a laborious task you returned to it enlivened. (4) You felt renewed and excited upon hearing a piece of good news.

After you access a renewed-energy experience, anchor the vigorous feeling when it's at its most intense level. Anchor it with a single image of that past experience, with a sound that occurred then, or with some natural physical gesture. Practice firing the anchor three or four times a day for a week or two until the anchor is thoroughly established. In the future, when fatigue sets in and you want to feel restored, fire the anchor.

Energy Visualization

Energy can be produced by visualizing metaphorically the processes that are necessary to bring the body from a fatigued state to a vigorous one. Without going into the details of physiology, the visualization consists of imagining (1) the distribution of oxygen, stored chemicals, and nutriments to the muscles; (2) the chemical activity that occurs within muscle cells; and (3) the elimination of waste products from the body.

The following is a metaphor of the activity of the human body that a number of athletes have found useful to maintain their energy levels, such as running long-distance races.

As if from a point up in space, they watch tankers (red blood cells) pick up oxygen gas from two storage depots (the lungs); seeing this, they feel their body becoming lighter as they breathe in. They watch the tankers travel upriver (the bloodstream) to a factory in which there are a storage tank (nutriments) and a central workroom full of machines (the muscles). They watch the tankers unload the oxygen, where it combines with the stored nutriments to become fuel for the muscles.

As the fuel is fed to the factory machines (the muscles), they see the levers working faster and smoother; while watching this, they imagine their muscles working more energetically. They also see smoke (expired air) coming out of the factory chimney and imagine getting rid of waste products from their body as they exhale.

Whenever you feel sluggish on the court—when your volleys lack zip or your play is lethargic—just run the tanker movie in your mind, feel yourself becoming lighter as you inhale, feel more energetic while you serve and return your opponent's shots, and, finally, imagine that you're blowing away the tiredness when you exhale. This metaphor is effective because it combines pictures of internal bodily activity with attention to breathing. One of the quickest ways to change your state of consciousness is to change your breathing—to increase its depth and to slow its rate.

Kristin Larkin, one of my graduate students at Columbia University and a personal fitness trainer in New York City, developed a rather interesting metaphorical movie for maintaining her energy level during workouts. The elements of her metaphor parallel the physiological action that goes on in active muscle cells. She uses the movie in her mind while doing heavy exercise. After practicing it several times while working out, she noticed that her energy increased; as a result she gained more confidence in the worth of the visualization process.

This is her metaphor:

"I see a picture of myself working out on a television screen in front of me [a metapicture]. Superimposed on that picture is another picture of a large muscle cell.

"As I watch the cell ignite into an orange flame [chemicals in the cell combine to create energy], the larger picture of myself is changing. I see many pockets of flame first multiplying in my legs and then spreading to all parts of my body. As my workout gets heavier, I see millions of flaming cells igniting. I also see my legs puffing up with energy, and the image of myself becomes superwoman.

"As I watch myself working, I notice a milky white substance [a buffering agent] mix with streams of yellow fluid [lactic acid] flowing from the flaming cells; this causes the yellow to fade away. Throughout the entire metaphor I imagine that I have more energy."

Kristin and I developed another metaphor that she uses for aerobics. She also recounts it to clients in her fitness classes. This metaphor is one that takes her back to her childhood. The idea of the metaphor is to get her to work *smoothly, strongly,* and in a *balanced* way when she's faced with increased activity. It involves eating fudge.

If you're a chocolate freak or have a weight problem, you might want to skip this one. If you decide to read on, eat fudge, and gain weight, you can blame it all on me.

"When I was a little girl, my mother used to make fudge and shared it with a neighbor. I'd be outside playing, and I could smell that fudge. I'd go inside and watch her stir it until it got creamy, smooth, and thick. Then she'd pour it into a big pan. After waiting until it hardened she'd cut it all up into nice bite sizes so some of it could be delivered to a neighbor.

"Then I'd get on my bike with the fudge in my basket. As

I pedaled up the hill to our neighbor's house, I could still smell the fudge. I looked forward to getting a piece of it when I got there."

Kristin interprets the metaphor in this way: The fudge represents her muscles—smooth, relaxed, and warm—while exercising (riding up the hill on her bike, which required balance and strength). The memory of her mother's fudge motivates her to work out in a smooth, relaxed, and balanced way. The good feeling of taking a gift to a neighbor generates a just-right state for her.

Evaluation

Although the energy anchor and the metaphorical movies have been effective for others, they may or may not work for you. An easy way to test them is to determine subjectively how energetic you feel, on a scale of 1 to 10, just before you use one of the techniques. Then rate how energetic you feel after anchoring or visualizing. If your energy has increased, the technique obviously worked.

Finally, notice the difference in the quality of your tennis game after applying these techniques. If your shots improve, find out if you can attribute the improvement to the exercises or to something else. These two tests are your best indicators of the validity of the techniques.

Pain Control

When pain is present, the appropriate action is to consult medical specialists to identify its cause and provide appropriate treatment and medication. If, however, chronic pain persists, you can learn how to reduce it while still undergoing medical treatment. Let's consider three pain-reducing techniques.

Inside Out

Inside Out is a technique that effectively reduces pain resulting from emotional stress, injury, or surgery. I've used it with hundreds of people. It's a very simple six-step process, as illustrated by the work I did with Gail, who complained of having a severe headache with no apparent cause.

"On a scale from zero to ten," I said, "rate the severity of the pain that you're experiencing right now."

"It's a doozy," she replied. "Ten!"

"What I want you to do," I instructed her, "is to imagine what that pain looks like. Describe it to me as if you were looking at it on the wall over there. In fact, project the image of your pain on the wall and tell me precisely what it looks like."

"What it looks like?" she asked, looking puzzled.

"Sure. Tell me its shape and how big it is."

Gail paused, stared at the wall, and then said, "It's shaped like a small football. It's expanding and contracting, as if it were being squeezed. That's the way it feels here in the back of my head."

"Fine description," I said. "Tell me about its color, texture, and density."

"It's glowing red. It's really heavy and seems to be filled with thick pieces of rubber. It's very smooth, like plastic."

"Can you see that smooth, pulsating, glowing red football filled with rubber on the wall right now?"

Gail nodded as her eyes focused on the wall.

"Hold that image there while doing something that may sound strange to you," I said. "Make a sound, either out loud or privately to yourself, that exactly matches the way your headache feels. Open your throat and let that feeling of pain come out."

Gail's eyes became unfocused as she uttered a rather feeble "Ow."

"Open your throat, Gail, and let that sound come out freely and strongly," I told her.

This time Gail wailed loudly. "Oooowwww!"

"That's right. Keep your throat open and adjust the sound so that it matches your pain."

After listening to her wail for about 10 seconds I interrupted her: "Stop the sound for a few seconds. In your peripheral vision, project another image on the wall, an image of a place of pleasure where you've been in the past. Put that picture on the left edge of your vision and keep the football image of your pain in the center."

"Okay, I've got the two pictures," she said.

I told her to start making the sound that matched her pain again and to keep it going. Then I instructed her to imagine a wind blowing from left to right across her pictures.

"Let the image of the pain vaporize and be blown away by the wind," I said, "as the picture of your place of pleasure moves to the center of your vision."

After about a minute Gail seemed to relax. Her posture slumped as her mouth opened and her chin dropped. "On a scale of zero to ten, what's the intensity of your pain now?"

She paused for a few seconds and then said, "Two. The headache's almost gone. That's amazing. Can I use that process for other headaches and other pains?"

I told her it can be used for any kind of pain anytime, but she should check out her headaches and other persistent pains with her doctor.

INSIDE OUT

1. Identify the precise location of your pain and rate its severity on a scale from zero to 10.

2. Project a clear image of the pain on a nearby surface. Identify its size, shape, density, weight, thickness, surface texture, and color.

3. Holding that image in view, make a sound that matches its intensity. The sound should express exactly how the pain feels. If it's inconvenient to utter the sound aloud, "hear" it loud and clear in your mind. Vary its pitch, tone, and volume until it matches the feeling and intensity of your pain.

4. In your peripheral vision to the left, project an image of a remembered place of pleasure.

5. Again focus on the projected image of pain, express what it feels like vocally or silently, and pretend that the pain image is vaporizing. As it disappears, gradually lower the sound and let the image of the place of pleasure move to the center of your vision.

6. Rate the severity of pain that remains on a scale from zero to 10. Compare it with the original rating in step 1.

The Inside Out technique usually reduces pain considerably or eliminates it altogether. Metaphorically you move the pain from inside your body to the outside, thus the title "Inside Out." The technique can be used almost anytime, and it's especially useful during a changeover between games. Just project an image of your pain onto a watercooler or onto an imaginary screen following the instructions above.

"Swish"

"Swish," described on page 85, can also be used to reduce or eliminate pain. An image of the painful state can be the large projected image used in the "Swish" process; it should be one color. A very small image representing the healed or painless state should be created and projected on top of the large image of pain at the seven o'clock position. The smaller second image should be another color.

To complete the "Swish" process, shrink the larger image until it fades away; at the same time increase the size of the small image until it's the only one remaining. Quickly repeat the "Swish" process five times, letting your mind go blank after each "Swish."

Self-Hypnosis

I learned a process of alleviating pain with self-hypnosis from a 12-year-old girl who suffered from sickle-cell anemia. It consists of imagining a dial with a control knob located on your mental screen. The dial indicates the intensity of a particular pain that you may have in a specific part of your body. The knob is used to regulate the intensity of the pain on the dial. As the needle on the dial registers the degree of pain, silently make a sound or tone that corresponds to the way the pain feels.

While you're in an altered state, see an imaginary strand of nerves that connects the painful area of your body to the dial. Experiment with regulating the intensity of the pain. Increase it by turning the knob under the dial in one direction; decrease it by turning the knob in the opposite direction. As the needle registers a higher intensity of pain, feel the pain increase and hear the sound become louder. Then turn the knob in the opposite direction to reduce the pain and volume of sound as much as possible. Bring yourself back from the altered state to "normal." The pain should be eliminated entirely or reduced to a tolerable level.

If you have various kinds of pain in different parts of your body, you can create a console of dials with each dial representing a specific pain. If you have more than one kind of pain, you can manipulate the appropriate dial for each of them.

Healing

During the last eight to ten years many books focusing on the mind-body relationship, especially as it relates to illness and healing, have been written for laymen. You might find some of them of particular interest: *Anatomy of an Illness* by Norman Cousins; *Getting Well Again* by Carl Simonton, a cancer specialist, and his associates; *Love, Medicine & Miracles* by Bernie Siegel, a surgeon; and *Minding the Body, Mending the Mind* by Joan Borysenko, director of the Mind/Body Clinic at Harvard Medical School. A more technical book that explains the theory behind mental healing is *The Psychobiology of Mind-Body Healing* by Ernest Rossi, a protégé of Dr. Milton Erickson.

Norman Cousins clearly demonstrates the power of his natural healing resources. Together with his doctor's medical expertise and encouragement and through humorous movies, books, and cartoons, he overcame his depression and disease. Laughter, and the positive emotional state it evoked, proved to be an important part of his cure.

Bernie Siegel and Carl Simonton have demonstrated the power of the mind as an adjunct to medical treatment for cancer patients. Joan Borysenko describes an extensive preventive medicine program of mental/emotional techniques to supplement medical treatment at Harvard.

According to respected scientists, we are able to heal ourselves by using mental processes. Simply stated, they believe that our thoughts and emotions affect body chemistry, especially hormones and neuropeptides. These chemicals affect our immune response to disease.

The essential elements of mental healing are a belief in your own power to heal yourself and your ability to accurately visualize the physiological healing processes that help the body repair itself with or without the use of medicine and surgery.

Here are some examples of how several of my clients hastened their healing with several metaskills techniques.

Torn Ankle Ligaments

Cynthia, a young figure skater who had orthopedic surgery for a serious foot injury, enhanced her recovery by her own unusual visualization process. She "saw" boatloads of little men in white hospital gowns traveling through her bloodstream to the site of the injury. They unloaded special ligament-stretching paraphernalia, sewing machines, and chemical nutriments. They then stretched the ligaments, sewed them securely to the bones in her foot, and sprinkled medicine on top of the ligaments.

She also visualized a crew of garbage men who cleaned up the waste left by her interior tailors and by the body's natural healing processes; they loaded the waste onto scows that were dispersed through her blood vessels to her liver, kidneys, intestines, and lungs for eventual disposal outside of her body.

Cynthia held her own matinee movies every day during

recovery. When she left the hospital, her doctor told her that she had recovered from the surgery in an amazingly short period of time.

Hay Fever

Another athlete created an internal movie to eliminate sneezing during the hay fever season. He imagines a team of men in white coats swabbing his sinus cavities with mops. Another team of men follows the first team and paints his sinus cavities with a molasses-type substance to prevent the infiltration of pollen and other irritating pollutants. The result: he stops sneezing, and his nasal passages clear up.

Knee Surgery

Here's a personal testimony. In the early 1970s I had surgery on my left knee for a torn ligament. Ten years later I had severe pain and limited movement in my right knee. The orthopedic surgeon who had diagnosed my injury and assisted in the left-knee surgery told me the same problem now existed in my right knee. He prescribed surgery identical to the previous procedure.

I told him I wanted to use visualization to heal my knee before I underwent any surgery. I asked him to describe fully what had to happen for my knee to heal naturally. Although he was extremely skeptical, as many orthopedists are, he told me what would have to happen inside the knee capsule. I left his office, and he wished me success.

I created a metaphorical movie to activate the healing process and watched it in my mind daily for a couple of weeks and then once a week for several months. It is now seven years later, and I no longer have pain. I had no surgery, and I'm as active as I was before my right knee acted up. I attribute this to my healing movie.

Below is a description of a simple visualization method of mental healing that I have developed and used successfully with scores of athletes; it doesn't always work. It's based primarily on Carl Simonton's work. You too can use it as a supplement to the treatment and medication prescribed by your physician. It consists of the following steps.

METASKILLS HEALING

1. Consult your physician and ask him to give you a complete and accurate description, in mechanical and chemical terms, of what must happen in your body to bring it back to normal, including the effects of medication on the healing processes. Make sure you understand exactly what that process is by restating to your doctor in your own words his or her description. When the doctor verifies your layman's description, it becomes the basis for creating your own mental-healing movie.

2. Create a movie that metaphorically represents the mechanical and chemical processes of healing. (For example, a balloon deflating could represent reduction in swelling; a weaver working on a loom could signify the rejoining of torn tissue.)

3. "Run" your movie several times a day. Include a segment in the movie that portrays you as gradually healing, regaining energy, and becoming physically active again.

4. After successful healing, praise yourself for the work you've done.

If your condition doesn't improve following a week or so of visualization, the process you've been using may need to be continued for several more weeks, or it may need to be changed. The ineffectiveness of your metaphorical movie could be the result of incomplete medical knowledge since physicians are not always totally sure of exactly how medications work or precisely how the body heals. Therefore, the movie may not represent the recovery process accurately.

If you see distorted images, hear muffled sounds, or feel uncomfortable as you watch, your unconscious mind may be indicating to you where your movie is inaccurate. Corrections, based on more knowledge from your doctor and better interpretation of that knowledge on your part, can be made in the movie wherever you experience distorted sensory information.

If your health status has not improved after changing the movie and watching it for several more weeks, it makes sense to abandon the process and perhaps see another doctor.

TEN

Game, Set, Match

How you think about the game of tennis, what you want to get from the participation, and how you think while you're actually playing tennis are equally important. In this chapter I'll present a few ideas to you about how you can achieve your most desired tennis outcomes, how you can free yourself to enjoy the game thoroughly, and how to get satisfaction from playing it. I'll discuss the value of having realistic expectations, and point out how you can overcome pressure. I'll also point out how you can identify your desired performance outcomes and select appropriate metaskills techniques to achieve them.

Expectations

Just how realistic are you about your tennis game? When you miss your second serve, net an easy forehand, or drive an overhead into the back fence, are you upset? Often when I hear irate tennis players muttering oaths to themselves or screaming in desperation over missing an easy lob, or see them slamming their racquets on the ground with rage, it looks and sounds as though they expect a whole lot more than is possible at the moment. It's as if they should be perfect and win every point.

Many athletes have told me that the best frame of mind for competing in any sport is the attitude of going out to have a good time. This is true for PGA Tour golfers, Olympic figure skaters, Grand Prix horseback riders, racquetball players, you name the sport. When having fun and playing as well as possible are the desired outcomes, it doesn't matter what the result of a match is; and more than likely the result will be a good one if you're enjoying the game.

Pressure

Do you feel pressure to win most of your matches? If you do, don't tell me it's pressure put on by competitors, spectators, the media, or family and friends. It's certainly a fact that some sportscasters think that any exceptional tour player, like Ivan Lendl, has a "monkey on his back" when he doesn't win a particular grand slam event. That is, they speculate that Lendl should feel pressure to win Wimbledon because of the common expectation in our society that he *should* win if he is to be considered "number one." Actually the sportswriters are projecting what they themselves might feel if they were in Lendl's sneakers. The press has done such a good job of convincing the public of this that even Lendl has "bought" their expectations. As a result he generates so much pressure within himself to win on grass that he "clutches" in England.

The fact of the matter is that you, and only you, generate the pressure you feel. You put the monkey on your own back by accepting the common value of *having* to win. In effect you let yourself become brainwashed. You don't *have* to win.

Here's a simple illustration of what I mean. An easy overhead is routine when you practice, but it can become a "pressure shot" and could eventually, if missed, turn into a tied-up match when you're up two sets in the fourth with games tied at five all. How is that pressure generated? From inside of you, by virtue of how you think. It could spring from a number of thoughts—your desire, if not compulsion, to put away a winner and feel satisfied, to please someone else, to get recognition, or just to win. If winning or playing each shot well is important but not absolutely essential, then *having* to make the overhead really doesn't matter, so the pressure is removed.

Winning

Many tennis players heap enormous pressure on themselves to win. Having to win, feeling *compelled* to win, is counterproductive because it generates muscle tension that interferes with swinging the racquet smoothly. *Wanting* to win out of genuine desire, on the other hand, serves as motivation to excel. When you excel, you present a better challenge to your opponents. I don't know very many athletes who want to compete with someone who doesn't play up to his potential.

I strongly believe that the better your opponent plays, the more opportunity you have to challenge yourself and dig deeper into your resources. In this way you really challenge your opponent. The better each of you plays, the better each of you can become. When a tennis match is played from this perspective, opponents become fellow competitors who appreciate each other; they aren't simply objects to be hated and defeated.

In my associations with fine athletes in many sports, nearly all of them say that when they play their best and win against topflight opponents, victory becomes a highly prized bonus—a bonus because of the satisfaction of reaching a personal-best performance goal. On the other hand, even if they lose under the same circumstances, they experience a bittersweet feeling—disappointment over the loss coupled with the satisfaction of having played well. In contrast they say that a victory that comes after playing poorly, irrespective of the opponent's quality of play, provides very little satisfaction.

If you find that you're feeling pressure to win, it might be important to ask yourself what would happen if you didn't win. What would you lose besides the match? Would you feel as if you were letting someone else down—your coach, your playing partner, your family or friends? Would letting them down make you feel bad?

If the answer is yes, it's quite likely that you're taking unrealistic responsibility for how others feel and getting your own sense of satisfaction from their approval instead of from yourself. This means that you're unnecessarily dependent on others for feeling good about how you play. You're playing a dependent mind game instead of taking full responsibility for your own actions and feelings. In other words, you're operating in your mind *as if* you were out there for someone else when actually you're not.

Let's face it. You don't play tennis, or do anything else for that matter, solely for another person. *Everything you do is for yourself.* Even when you do something to please someone else, you do it because *you* get something in return—enjoyment from playing the game, love, recognition, money, whatever—or you do what you do to avoid something such as criticism or punishment.

What else might happen if you didn't win? Would you feel

embarrassed? Would you feel inadequate as a person? Would you feel dissatisfied with yourself? If your answer to these questions is yes, then your chances of feeling good about yourself are dim since only one player wins a tournament; the rest lose. One person wins the ladies' singles at Wimbledon; 127 women lose. Unfortunately the we're-number-one mania in the sports world is another kind of "mind game" that feeds an irrational sense of the value of a scoreboard victory.

The true measure of the worth of your tennis game and yourself is how you feel about your own efforts. If you believe you really applied yourself, irrespective of the score, that's all that anyone can ask. It's natural to feel disappointment over poor play. However, feeling embarrassed with your game implies a low sense of self-esteem because you allow spectators to determine your self-worth.

So wanting to win creates a paradox. If you try too hard, if you're *compelled* to win, you'll generate pressure that results in poor play; if you minimize winning and tell yourself just to enjoy playing, it's highly likely that you'll play well and have a better chance to win. When you enjoy yourself and—incidentally—win, it feeds your sense of accomplishment, satisfaction, and self-worth.

"Shouldniks"

It's easy to spot dependent, compulsive people who put tremendous pressure on themselves to win or play perfectly. Just listen to their language. They use phrases containing "need to," "must," "got to," "have to," or "should": "I've *got to* practice my backhands"; "I *should* get all my first serves in"; "I *should* have hit it deep"; or "I've *got to* follow through on my forehand." When unforced errors are examined carefully, I'd bet that most of them arise from being what I call a "shouldnik."

There's a very simple way to eliminate the internal mind game that creates such pressure. It merely involves substituting the phrase. "I *want* to do X because . . ." for the words "I *must* or *should* do X." When you say "want" with conviction, followed by a reason, you take full responsibility for your wishes and actions. As a result, you'll release a source of energy and motivation to accomplish X, or you'll realize that you're incapable of doing X, or you'll decide you don't want to do it at all.

Here's an assignment. Make sure you follow it exactly! If you already feel pressure to comply with my command, you'll know that you have a tendency to be a "shouldnik," and this exercise may help you overcome it. For two weeks I encourage you to become acutely aware of every time you say "I should" or its equivalent. When you consciously hear it, pay careful attention to how you feel inside—your bodily sensations—just after you admonish yourself. Then substitute the word "want" for "should" and pay attention again to the physical sensations in your body. Compare the two kinds of sensations and notice the difference between them.

Do an exercise with me now. Say to yourself with conviction, "I should [insert something you've been putting off, such as practicing overheads, working on your net game, cutting the grass, balancing the checkbook, washing windows, writing to so-and-so]." What does it feel like in your body when you say this? Make a mental note of the physical feelings.

Now say to yourself, "I *want* to [insert what you said you should do]," paying close attention to the bodily sensations that are generated as you think about doing it. Are the "want" feelings different from the "should" feelings? Do you still want to do it? Are you more determined than before to do it?

Do you want to get someone else to do it for you? Or do you want to scrap the whole idea?

I can almost guarantee that if you use this exercise faithfully for two full weeks—substituting "want" for every time you say "should"—you'll feel much differently about yourself and your life. If you feel that you *should* complete this assignment, ask yourself if you really want to. It's important that you do it out of desire, not compulsion.

Perfectionism

Frequently "shouldniks" are perfectionists. Perfectionists are people who leave no stone unturned to make whatever they do absolutely perfect, without flaw. They are relentless. Please don't misunderstand me. Doing things superbly and paying attention to detail is very important. The point I want to make about perfectionism is that it's the compulsion that things *must* be just so that generates the pressure in yourself to perform beyond *anyone's* capability, let alone your own.

I'm reminded of a client of mine, a golf professional, who reframed his own dogged determination to play perfectly. He gave himself permission to make mistakes on the golf course since they were inevitable. He anchored this error-accepting state by carrying a South African golf pencil in his pocket when he competes. South African pencils, unlike U.S. golf pencils, have erasers on them.

Instead of shouting epithets and using racquets as hatchets to scar the court when you make an unforced error, you have another choice of behavior. If the error is, indeed, unforced, then obviously you are capable of making the shot you missed. To scold yourself and dwell on the mistake in your mind is counterproductive. First, you generate tension in your muscles that interferes with stroking the ball smoothly. Second, you etch in your nerves and muscles a program to repeat the error. And third, you are being rude to your opponent, who actually *may* have forced the error.

You have at least one other choice when you make an unforced error. Merely say to yourself, "I can make that shot," and picture in your mind hitting the ball correctly and feeling in your muscles what it's like to make the right kind of stroke. Immediately return to the baseline and swish your mind to blank, ready for the next point. At the next practice session you can spend some time working on correcting the goof. Thinking about it during a match reinforces the error.

Establishing Desired Outcomes

Since you can't play perfectly, what is it that you want to achieve in tennis? Part of the metaskills approach is to use a systematic way of deciding what's worth achieving—your outcomes—and how you can get them with various techniques. This is accomplished by following some basic principles.

Principle of Positivity

Whenever tennis players come to me for help, my first question is "What do you want to accomplish?" Invariably they begin by telling me what's the matter with their game and what they don't want. Since this approach is usually, but not always, self-defeating, I play a mind game with them. Let's try an experiment right now to illustrate a very important point that could make your tennis game so much better with very little work.

In about 10 seconds I'm going to tell you to do something. At that time pay attention to what you experience inside— what you see and hear in your mind and what you feel in your muscles and other parts of your body. Get ready to follow my instructions. Here goes: Don't be aware of your breathing right now.

What happened inside? If you're a normal human being, you automatically paid attention to your breathing. Perhaps you felt the rise and fall of your chest and the movement of your abdomen as you inhaled and exhaled. Perhaps you heard the sound of air in your nostrils. If not, check again to see if you're still alive. If so, how come you became aware of your breathing when I told you *not* to?

To understand my direction *not* to pay attention to your breathing, you *had* to turn your mind to the act of breathing. The reason you couldn't *not* become aware of your breathing is the fact that language, the nervous system, and the muscles are "wired" together, and words like *not* and *don't* are totally ignored. In other words, the nervous system knows no negation.

If you say to yourself, "Don't hit the ball into the net," you will access, consciously or unconsciously, a memory of having netted the ball in the past. The neural pathways between your brain and the muscles that control a poor shot will be activated automatically, probably without your being aware of it. Consequently you'll more than likely net the ball.

Of course you can block this by consciously rehearsing a good crosscourt shot in your mind while taking a proper practice swing. There are many people who consistently process information, consciously or unconsciously, by bring- ing counterexamples—opposites—to mind. Some of those people first think about what they don't want—hitting the ball in the net—and then shift automatically to thinking about what they do want. Others first think about how they want to hit the ball, yet unconsciously shift to thinking about how they don't want to hit it. This form of unconscious thinking can be devastating to your tennis game if you're not aware of it.

As you think about your tennis game right now, consider what you want to be able to do. If you find yourself saying something like "I don't want to hit so many sitters," just turn it around and say, "I want to hit sharp, crisp shots deep to the baseline." Do you feel different inside when you say this?

Principle of Specificity

The more you know precisely what you want to accomplish or do, the easier it will be to get it. You could say, "I want to be able to slice my backhands consistently." That statement can be further specified to include a more precise definition of "consistently," such as hitting them well 8 out of 10 times during competition.

The statement can be refined still further by identifying, in sensory-specific terms, what you would see, hear, and feel as you execute those backhands well. For example, you might want to change your stance; you might want to modify the swing path of the racquet; you might want to adjust your grip and lengthen or shorten your backswing; you might want to hear a certain kind of "brush" when the racquet strikes the ball; or you might want to visualize a certain kind of trajectory the ball will follow.

Sometimes it's hard to pinpoint how your preparation or stroke could be changed to improve your game. This is especially true for highly skilled players because everything is so grooved. The clue to your corrections is often reflected in language, especially the verbs, adverbs, and adjectives used to describe a swing problem.

Once when I was working with a tennis player, she said to me, "My forehand stroke doesn't feel rhythmical." This statement suggested that there were both kinesthetic (feel) and auditory (rhythmical) components to her swing analysis.

"Which muscles specifically don't *feel* right, and what kind of *sound* would you like to go along with your stroke?" I asked.

She swung her racquet a few times. "Oh, now I know what it is," she answered. "My backswing feels hurried. It lacks the smoothness when I stroke the ball the way I want to. I'm not humming a tune the way I usually do when I'm playing well. Let me do it again with a song in mind."

She hummed to herself as she hit a few ground strokes and said, "Now it feels the way I want it to."

My work with her was finished. I had just pointed her in the direction of her own knowledge. Metaskills techniques do exactly that.

The Backup Process

There's another way to uncover unknown elements of your game in need of refinement. It's the Backup Process, described on page 92. As you may recall, it consists of mentally rehearsing your *anticipated* performance in a *forthcoming* match against a specific opponent. By playing an entire match in your mind you can uncover defects in your game. These can become the basis for establishing your immediate desired outcomes.

Principle of Ecology

Everything with which human beings interact has a definite impact on their well-being. There is an interdependence among our beliefs, behaviors, expectations, nutrition, health, personal relationships, and the environment. Change any one of these elements and it could have a powerful effect on each of the others. Here are some examples.

Recently a woman told me that she had improved her tennis game so much that her husband felt threatened by it. Because she played better than he did, they began to quarrel on the court during mixed doubles matches.

A young player with professional tour ambitions discovered that he was spending so much time practicing that it took time away from his family. He began to realize that professional tennis would interfere with being the kind of husband and father he wanted to be. As a result he revised his career goals and is now in training to become an investment banker.

In another instance, a tour player changed his perspective about how he trained and dramatically improved his game. Instead of dedicating himself to grueling practice sessions, he adopted a laid-back attitude. When he was training intensely, his victories and earnings on the tour were almost nil. When he loosened up, he "came back" and won.

A young college player, while exploring how to improve his serve and volley, realized that it would take a lot of practice to adjust his serving footwork so that he could get to the net more quickly. He then weighed tennis practice time against academic study time; he realized how conflicted he was about what he really wanted—to go on tour or to finish his college education.

These examples demonstrate the importance of paying close attention to the ecology of your life whenever you make changes in the way you play tennis.

You can determine the ecological soundness of any desired outcome by answering two sets of important questions:

- What will achieving a particular outcome do for you? What will be the outcomes of that outcome?
- What's the worst that could happen if you achieve your desired outcome? Can you think of any reason why

achieving the desired outcome would *not* be in your best interests?

By answering these questions you will identify the potential positive and negative effects of achieving an outcome *before* you pursue it. By doing this you will either become more strongly motivated to achieve it or realize that its achievement may not be worth the effort. In both cases you'll save time and energy and avoid potential disappointment and disruption in your life.

Here are the steps to follow to establish ecological desired outcomes. Knowing them, you'll be ready to select the appropriate metaskills techniques to achieve them.

ESTABLISHING DESIRED OUTCOMES

1. Identify a shot (a desired outcome) that you want to learn or improve. Do this by using the Backup Process on page 92 to analyze your performance, or consult with your pro.

2. State your desired outcome in positive terms. Indicate what you want, not what you don't want (principle of positivity).

3. Identify and evaluate the potential positive and negative consequences of achieving a desired outcome *before* you pursue it. If your evaluation is positive, continue to the next step. If not, go back to step 1 and identify another desired outcome (principle of ecology).

4. Define your desired outcome in precise sensory terms, knowing what you will see, hear, and feel when your desired outcome has been achieved (principle of specificity).

Going for It

Achieving positive ecological outcomes through metaskills techniques can be simple if you go for them one at a time. Just pay attention to only one or two elements of each stroke until each becomes automatic, that is, until it becomes regulated by your unconscious mind. Similarly, focus on individual parts of your game strategy until they become grooved. They can eventually be woven into complete game plans for different opponents. Work with only one metaskills technique at a time. Gradually you will learn to swing your mind and your moods so that you can swing your racquet better from all parts of the court.

But which metaskills techniques are most appropriate for your specific desired outcomes? I have prepared an outline with page references in Appendix C that briefly describes the purposes of each technique and which ones can be used to achieve various desired outcomes. It serves as a quick reference to help you select the technique most appropriate for the particular outcome you have in mind. Frequently more than one technique can be used to achieve a desired outcome; and most techniques can be applied to achieve a number of different outcomes.

I suggest that you use my techniques experimentally. By that I mean fully commit yourself to following the steps of each technique several times exactly as presented. While doing this, notice what happens to your performance. When one technique doesn't work, use another.

After each practice session and each match, ask yourself the question "What did I learn?" regardless of the results. I really want you to think deeply about what you learn about yourself—your moods, the way you think, the things you value, and the way you feel about life and tennis. Then truly honor what you've discovered about your inner self. Once you know and honor yourself, you can let your unconscious mind do all the work on the court while your conscious mind enjoys the playing.

When you truly honor yourself, you will be free of internal conflicts that sap energy and interfere with performance. Without self-knowledge and acceptance you'll be playing against two opponents, the person across the net and your inner self. When you overcome your inner opponent, when you know and accept yourself, winning matches becomes less important because you have won the inner victory, the challenge that faces all of us. And paradoxically, you may discover that you will win more often.

APPENDIX A

Uptime Cues

The following list of "uptime" visual, kinesthetic, and auditory cues constitutes the sensory information that tennis players have found useful in regulating their game.

Visual

Court line markings
Net cord
Net posts
Movement of leaves in trees created by the wind
Movement of flags created by the wind
Location of the east–west direction
Debris on the playing surface
Shadows on the playing surface
The tennis ball itself
Seams of the ball
Trajectory of ball's flight
Angle of ball's bounce from ground

Spin of ball

The back surface of the ball during the serve

The target: the area within the opponent's court to which the ball will be hit

Broken racquet strings

Alignment of racquet face with respect to the target and ball at impact

Alignment of racquet face with respect to the ball and parts of the body (e.g., shoulders, hips, hands) at impact

Level of racquet head in relation to the hands throughout entire swing

Path of racquet head throughout the entire swing

Position of hands in relation to the racquet face and ball at time of impact

Position of hands on the grip

Position of elbows throughout the swing

Position of the shoulders in relation to the target

Position of body in relation to the ball

Position of feet in relation to the ball

Position of feet in relation to the target

Position of the hips and abdomen at the finish of the follow-through

Position of hands and racquet at the finish of the follow-through

Position of the shoulders at the finish of the follow-through

Position of the racquet face while waiting at the net

Location of ball release on serve

Height of tossed ball at impact on the serve

Vertical movement of ball-tossing hand

Position of free arm during preparation for an overhead

Position of self on the court

Position of opponent on the court

Open space on the court

Timing and speed of opponent's backswing

Position of opponent's racquet face at impact

Position of opponent's feet and shoulders
Position of opponent's wrist and forearm at impact
Quickness of opponent's movement on the court
Opponent's grip
Opponent's facial expressions
Opponent's posture

Auditory

"Whoosh" of racquet during swing
Ball striking your own and opponent's racquet strings
Ball hitting court
Ball hitting net cord
Officials' voices
Your own breathing
Opponent's breathing
Footsteps of self and opponent on the playing surface
Wind in the trees
Wind across your ears

Kinesthetic

Speed of movement toward the ball
Knee flexion
Straightness of back
Softness of grip
Tension of grip
Flexibility of wrists
Rotation of wrists
Firmness of wrists
Tension of fingers on the racquet
Weight of racquet

Roughness of racquet grip

Surface of the balls

Sensitivity to distribution of weight during execution of a shot

Sensitivity to balance during execution of a shot

Length of backswing

Sensitivity of fingers

Tension/relaxation of wrist and arm muscles

Tension/relaxation of shoulders and neck

Tension/relaxation of legs

Degree of elbow bend

Wrist rotation

Wrist flexibility

Rotation of the shoulders, trunk, and hips

Acceleration of the racquet head at impact

Impact of racquet face on the ball

Position of hands during the follow-through

Extent of the "finish" of the arms at the end of the follow-through

Weight shift during strokes

Friction of court surface on bottom of tennis shoes

Softness/hardness of playing surface

Movement of air over skin (wind)

Ambient air temperature on the skin

Sensory Awareness

This appendix contains two parts: (1) a series of questions that identify how people internally represent their sensory experience and (2) exercises designed to strengthen sensory awareness.

Representation of Sensory Experience

The questions that follow are a modification of what Richard Bandler and Will MacDonald presented in their book *An Insider's Guide to Sub-Modalities*. Submodalities are classified according to each of the three main channels of awareness that are crucial for regulating athletic skills: vision, audition (hearing), and kinesthesia (feeling). The senses of smell and taste are of little consequence in sports, except when fear is involved. Then both smell and taste seem to be quite important.

These questions can serve as a handy reference when

you're practicing several metaskills techniques: Sherlock Holmes Exercise, uptime anchor, just-right anchors, Discovering Differences, "Swish," and self-hypnosis. Whenever the instructions for any of these techniques tell you to change *how* you see, hear, and feel "on the inside" or in your mind, the questions below can help you do just that.

Vision

Brightness: Are the images brighter than normal, with lots of light, or are they dark? Are some images brighter than others?

Color: Are images in color or only in black and white? Is there a full spectrum of color, or is there a dominance of one or more colors?

Contrast: Is there a sharp contrast in the objects and colors, or are they subdued or washed out?

Focus: Are the images sharply focused or fuzzy?

Distance: Are you looking at the image as if zoomed in, or do you have a wide-angle view? How wide is the angle?

Location: Where is the image located in space? Is it within your head? Or is it located outside of you—to the front, side, rear, down, up? How far away is it (in feet and inches)? Does the screen on which the image is projected move? If so, in what direction?

Size: How big is the image (approximately, in inches or feet)? Does the size change?

Shape: Is the image round, square, triangular, rectangular?

Border: Does the image have a frame or border? Describe the size and design of the border.

Viewpoint: Are you seeing yourself in the picture as if you were a spectator, or are you seeing what you would normally see if you were actually there in that place at that time? From what direction are you looking at yourself—from the side (right or left), back, front, above, at an angle? Is the image tilted at an angle from front to back or from side to side? Does the image seem to wrap around you, or is it flat or two-dimensional?

Motion: Is the image a still picture, or are you watching a movie? Is there a series of images, like slides flashing on the screen one by one? Do you see multiple still pictures at the same time or all at once? If you're seeing a movie, is it like a loop film, running over and over again? How fast are the motion pictures moving—at normal speed, slower than normal, or faster than normal?

Number: How many images are there? Are they separate? Superimposed? Are they side by side or arranged vertically?

Audition (Hearing)

Volume: How loud is the sound? Is it normal, above normal, or below normal?

Duration: Does the sound persist continuously, or is it intermittent?

Pitch: Are the sounds high- or low-pitched? Is the pitch higher or lower than normal?

Tone: Are the sounds thin, full, rich, grating, harsh, pleasant, resonant?

Melody: Is the sound harmonious, discordant, monotone?

Tempo: Is the beat fast or slow?

Rhythm: Is the rhythm syncopated or even-cadenced?

Location: Where is the source of the sound located? At a particular point within your body? Outside your body? Where, specifically, is the source of the sound located outside your body?

Direction: In what direction does the sound flow? Does it flow from inside out, outside in, upward, downward? Is the sound stereophonic, or do you hear it from only one direction?

Background: Are there background noises? If so, ask the questions above.

Kinesthesia (Feeling)

It's important to distinguish the feelings that signify an emotional state as contrasted with the feelings of skillful movement performance. Movement can be more or less skillful, depending on the nature of the emotional state. Each of the categories below applies to both skillful performance and emotional states.

Location: Where, specifically, in your body do you feel the sensations? Does the feeling remain in one place, or does it spread? Is the feeling localized, diffused, or the same throughout your body? Is there a difference in feelings on each side of your body? Is there a difference in feelings in the upper half as contrasted with the lower half of your body?

Duration: Do the feelings persist, or are they intermittent?

Characterization: How would you describe the quality of the feelings? Warm/cold? Relaxed/tense? Heavy/light? Extended/contracted? Even/pulsating? Strong/weak?

Movement: How would you describe the nature of your movements? Strong/weak? Coordinated/disjointed? Gentle/ballistic? Smooth/jerky? Flexible/limited? Relaxed/tense? Slow/quick? Balanced/unbalanced?

Intensity: How strong are the sensations? What is the degree of strength, power, balance, relaxation, flexibility, smoothness, warmth, lightness, coordination in relation to normal?

Sensory Awareness Exercises

Few people process visual, auditory, and kinesthetic information equally well. Most of us are strong in the use of one or two sensory systems and weak in others. The exercises that follow are designed to strengthen your weaker senses. Most of the exercises can be done at any time, anywhere— while on the court, riding to work, listening to a boring lecture, showering, cutting the grass, or waiting for a court to become vacant.

These exercises are merely examples of a few ways to improve your sensory awareness; use your ingenuity to create others.

Crossover Training

Crossover training is a series of exercises that make use of the natural, inborn synesthesia "wiring" in your brain and nervous system. They capitalize on the strength of your most sensitive sensory channel as a way to build up your sensitivity in other channels.

Crossover from Hearing to Other Channels
Hear a bird sing and make a *picture* of a bird in your mind. *Hear* an automobile horn and *feel* the vibrations of the horn in some part of your body. In your mind, *hear* the *"brush"* of a past slice shot and *feel* the swing that put the ball down the line.

Crossover from Feeling to Other Channels
When you *feel* anger, see a *color.* Convert a painful *feeling* into the *sound* "Ouch!" While *feeling* the actual swing of your racquet, generate in your mind's eye an *image* of a ball going into the corner of your opponent's court.

Crossover from Seeing to Other Channels
Make an internal *image* of a fire engine and *hear* its siren in your mind. Make a picture in your mind of a pleasant *scene*

and pay attention to where in your body you have a pleasant *feeling*. *Observe* someone lifting something heavy and *feel* the strain of the muscular effort involved in your own muscles. Create an internal *image* of a player serving and *hear* in your mind the sound of the racquet strike the ball. Remember the *trajectory* of a fine lob and *feel* the swing that produced it.

Watch the reflection of yourself tossing a ball while preparing to serve in a mirror or glass patio door, paying particular attention to various elements of the preparation and ball-tossing action—the position of your entire body, for instance, or the movement of the tossing hand and arm. When you *see* that the tossing action is correct, pay attention to the *muscle feelings* associated with it. Close your eyes and reproduce the ball toss and feelings several times. Open your eyes and check the movement in the mirror or glass door. Repeat this exercise until you're sure you have the muscle feelings of the proper ball-tossing action without having to rely on the reflections.

Visual Imagery

Internal visual imagery is central to playing tennis well. It prepares you mentally for each shot and helps you analyze and correct your form. The exercises below are designed to increase your internal visual skills.

Making Metapictures

A metapicture is an internal image in which you see yourself as if you were looking through someone else's eyes, like watching yourself swing a racquet on videotape. This is an important imagery skill because it helps you evaluate your own swinging movements.

- Seated comfortably in a chair, wiggle your toes and feel your feet on the floor. Now make a picture of only your feet. Next, move your lower leg and make a picture of it from the knee down; connect that picture to the one of your feet. Next, contract your thigh muscles, move your leg, and make a picture of your thigh; connect that picture to the previous picture of your lower legs and feet. Continue until you have connected all of you together. Don't forget your head. By this time you should have a complete metapicture of yourself.

- Practice making metapictures of yourself while swinging a racquet for various shots. Become very sensitive to what each part of your body is doing throughout each swing—head, shoulders, arms, hands, torso, hips, legs, feet.

- Watch a portion of a videotaped recording of, for example, a pro's forehand topspin. Stop the tape, close your eyes, and visually reproduce the same shot in your mind. Replay the videotape to determine the accuracy of your internal movie. Adjust your internal images until they match the forehand on the video screen.

Making Superimposed Pictures and Multiple Images

- Project onto the surface of an actual tennis court an imaginary moving picture of a tennis ball flying directly into a corner of the opponent's service box.

- On an imaginary screen located within your head, project four slide pictures of your backhand stroke; the slides consist of the backswing, the forward movement of the racquet toward the ball, the position of the racquet head at impact, and the follow-through position. Use these mental slides as a guide for practicing the backhand.

- Make a movie of a particular shot in your mind's eye and vary its brightness, sharpness, size, color, and focus. Notice what effect these variations have on the imaginary shot.

Auditory Awareness

I'm sure you realize that there are times during practice and a match when you talk to yourself or hear the voices of others in your mind telling you what to do or what not to do. They can be useful when they're in your control or a hindrance when they're not. Similarly external noises can be distracting when you're making a shot unless you know how to tune them out or use them constructively. Below are exercises to increase your sensitivity to sounds; make use of them in your mind to improve your tennis game.

External Auditory

- Listen to the voice of someone on radio or television; turn off the sound and mimic the tone, volume, and syntax of the voice; turn the sound back on and compare the sound of your own voice with the one you heard. Repeat this process until you can mimic the voice as well as possible.
- Mimic as well as you can the sounds of animals as you hear them—a bird singing, for example, or a dog barking.
- Listen intently to a distracting sound while hitting a tennis ball. Notice the quality of the shot. Now pretend the distracting sound is entering your muscles, creating energy in your body and making your stroke more powerful. Notice the quality of the shot. Is there a difference?

- Listen intently to a distracting sound as you are preparing to make a shot. Immediately shift your attention to closely watching the spin of the ball. Make the shot as you focus intently on the spin. Notice the quality of the shot. Reflect on what happened to the distracting sound.

Internal Auditory

- Modify the volume and tone of your own or someone else's voice that you hear inside your head. Vary the nature of the internal voice from loud, harsh, and critical to soft, pleasant, and supportive. Notice how your bodily sensations vary with the change in tone and volume.
- When you hear an internal critical voice, substitute pleasant music. Notice any change in physical tension.
- Deliberately talk to yourself *while* serving and notice the quality of the serve. Then quiet your mind, serve another ball, and notice the quality of that serve. Is there a difference?
- Immediately after making a poor shot, deliberately criticize yourself harshly in your mind and notice the amount of tension in your body. Then stop criticizing yourself and without further thought hit another ball. Notice the quality of that shot. Was the second shot better or worse than the first? If better, perhaps you were too tense on the first shot; if worse, perhaps you became too relaxed.
- Now change the internal critical voice to a calm, supportive one, giving yourself positive instructions about stroking the ball well. How much physical tension do you feel when you change your internal voice from being critical to supportive?

Kinesthetic Awareness

Contrary to logical expectations, I have found that many athletes are largely unaware of their bodily sensations. Tennis players in particular are insensitive to the specific muscle tensions involved in hitting a ball, and they are unaware of the bodily sensations that are linked to their emotional states when they are playing a point. Lacking these sensitivities, players are missing important information that could improve their game immensely. For example, if you're unaware of the amount of tension in your hands, wrists, and forearms, it will be difficult to control the path of the racquet head. The exercises below are designed to refine your awareness of physical tensions and emotion because they have a direct bearing on the smoothness and rhythm of your shots.

Body Scanning

Several times a day, stop doing whatever you are doing and pay attention to the amount of tension/relaxation and warmth/coolness that exist in various parts of your body—head, neck, shoulders, arms, wrists, hands, fingers, chest, abdomen, back, hips, thighs, knees, calves, ankles, feet, toes.

Physical Sensations Related
to Swinging a Tennis Racquet

- Increase and decrease the amount of tension in your hands, wrists, and forearms separately as you make a number of shots; the tension should vary from very loose to very tight. Notice the quality of the shots as you vary the tension.
- Immediately after making a fine shot, reproduce the swing and become aware of the amount of tension you feel in your legs, shoulders, hands, wrists, and fore-

arms. Do the same thing after making a poor shot. Determine the differences in muscle tension between the good and bad shot.

Emotional Awareness

You probably know that emotions affect muscle tension and therefore are linked closely to the way you make a particular shot. Emotional states can either facilitate or disrupt your game. Anger at yourself after making an unforced error usually increases muscle tension in your hands and wrists, causing you to grasp the racquet in a death grip. Muscle tension can also affect the tempo of your stroke. In both cases the quality of a shot is affected. The following exercises will help you increase your emotional awareness.

- Each time you become aware of a strong emotion on the tennis court, scan your body to identify the specific physical sensations that accompany it. For example, clenched fists suggest anger, butterflies in the stomach usually mean fear, and tightness in the leg muscles could mean frustration. Notice the most intense sensations related to each emotional state and how that tension affects the quality of your shots.
- Experiment with increasing and then decreasing tension in the muscles associated with a particular emotion identified in the previous exercise. Is there any change in your emotional state? Again notice how it affects various shots.
- When an emotion—for instance, anger, frustration, worry, or fear—becomes too strong during a match, decrease tension in the muscles associated with the emotion, look upward, and make an internal image of a pleasant scene. Is there a reduction in emotional intensity? Do your shots improve?

Guide to Selecting Metaskills Techniques

This appendix is a ready reference and guide to selecting appropriate metaskills techniques to achieve various desired outcomes. It contains two parts: (1) an alphabetical listing of the techniques and the purposes they serve and (2) an alphabetical listing of common desired outcomes and the techniques that can be used to achieve them.

For detailed information about each technique, refer to the pages in parentheses. You may also use the index to locate anecdotes related to the various techniques.

Techniques and the Purposes They Serve

Anchoring (p. 41)

Improve memory
Stabilize a state of consciousness
Change a state of consciousness quickly
Apply inner resources
Improve concentration
Increase confidence
Increase energy
Facilitate unconscious control of performance
Increase consistency of performance

Backup Process (p. 92)

Identify outcomes
Prepare for matches
Analyze performance

Body Scanning (p. 170)

Increase awareness of emotional states
Increase ability to analyze performance
Facilitate use of uptime anchor
Facilitate use of Discovering Difference

Colored-Image Anchor (p. 81)

Maintain consistency of performance
Stabilize emotional state

Competitive-State Anchor (p. 64)

Control anxiety during competition
Maintain an optimum competitive state
Prepare for a forthcoming match

Counting Process (p. 78)

Regulate stroke tempo

Crossover Training (p. 165)

Improve capacity to make internal images
Increase sensitivity to bodily sensations
Increase sensitivity to sound
Improve capacity to become aware of internal dialogue

Discovering Difference (p. 97)

Reduce confusion
Increase consistency of performance
Identify significant performance keys

Energy Anchor (p. 127)

Maintain an energized state
Overcome fatigue

Energy Visualization (p. 127)

Establish and maintain an energized state
Speed up recovery from fatigue

Establishing Desired Outcomes (p. 153)

Identify worthwhile outcomes
Specify precisely what you want to accomplish
Develop positive outlook
Maintain focused practice sessions

Free-Swing Anchor (p. 86)

Control stroke effort
Regulate stroke tempo
Stabilize emotional state
Increase consistency of performance

Get-It Process (p. 101)

Learn new shots
Improve shots

Get-It-Back Process (p. 104)

Relearn shots

Holographic Viewing (p. 105)

Analyze performance
Acquire new skills
Improve existing skills

Inside Out (p. 133)

Reduce or eliminate pain.

Mechanical Just-Right Anchor (p. 55)

Increase consistency of performance
Increase concentration

M & M Process (p. 75)

Change emotional state quickly
Stabilize emotional state
Establish and maintain stroke tempo
Establish and maintain playing pace
Increase consistency of performance

Metaskills Healing (p. 138)

Speed up healing
Heal without surgery or medication

Metapictures (p. 166)

Analyze performance
Reduce intensity of uncomfortable feelings
Gain a new perspective

Using Metaphors (p. 103)

Improve concentration
Maintain consistency
Create optimal performance state
Regulate energy level

Multiple Images (p. 167)

Improve consistency of performance

Off-Ramp Technique (p. 78)

Regulate stroke tempo

Paradoxical Intention (p. 106)

Increase consistency of performance
Increase confidence

Personal Power Anchor (p. 69)

Overcome anxiety
Tap resources of excellence and effectiveness
Build confidence

Tennis Resource Anchor (p. 62)

Improve shot
Increase consistency of performance

Self-Hypnosis (Betty Erickson Technique) (pp. 114, 123)

Maintain concentration
Develop relaxed state
Access long-forgotten experiences
Control pain
Create a just-right state
Distort perception of time
Access mental strategies
Facilitate healing

Build trust in the unconscious mind
Change unwanted habit patterns
Improve performance
Analyze performance
Build confidence

Sherlock Holmes Exercise (p. 22)

Understand how you process information
Analyze how you mentally regulate playing the game
Identify elements of mental strategies
Improve memory
Identify internal resources from past experiences
Recall past shots
Identify important performance keys
Identify just-right states
Facilitate getting into an altered state

"Shouldniks" (p. 145)

Reduce compulsive behavior
Identify worthwhile desired outcomes

"Swish" (p. 85)

Change emotional state
Reduce or eliminate pain

Uptime Anchor (p. 53)

Identify important performance keys
Increase concentration
Increase consistency of performance

Video Observation (p. 122)

Analyze performance
Increase consistency
Learn new shots

Desired Outcomes and the Techniques to Use

Below is a list of typical desired outcomes and the metaskills techniques that can be used to achieve them.

Anxiety Control

Competitive-state anchor
Just-right anchors
Personal power anchor
Self-hypnosis
"Swish"

Concentration

Discovering Difference
M & M Process
Metaphors
Self-hypnosis
Uptime anchor

Confidence

Competitive-state anchor
Resource anchor
Paradoxical intention
Personal power anchor
Self-hypnosis

Confusion, Reducing

Discovering Difference
Establishing desired outcomes
Uptime anchor

Consistency of Performance

Colored-image anchor

Competitive-state anchor
Discovering Difference
Mechanical just-right anchor
Uptime anchor
Video observation

Fatigue, Reducing

Energy anchor
Energy visualization

Healing

Metaskills healing
Self-hypnosis

Improving shots

Backup Process
Get-It-Back Process
Holographic viewing
Just-right anchors
Sherlock Holmes Exercise
Video observation

Learning new shots

Get-It Process
Holographic viewing
Video observation

Outcomes, Determining

Backup Process
Establishing desired outcomes

Pain Control

Inside Out
Self-hypnosis
"Swish"

Shot Analysis

Backup Process
Discovering Difference
Holographic viewing
Metapictures
Self-hypnosis
Sherlock Holmes Exercise
Uptime anchor
Video observation

State change

Energy anchor
Just-right anchors
M & M Process
Metapictures
Self-hypnosis
"Swish"

Stabilize State

Anchoring
M & M Process
Metaphors
"Swish"

Stroke Tempo

Counting Process
M & M Process
Metaphors
Off-Ramp Technique
Video observation

Tournament and Match Preparation

Backup Process
Competitive-state anchor
Self-hypnosis
Video observation

Selected References: Neuro-Linguistic Programming

Andreas, Connirae, and Steve Andreas. *Heart of the Mind.* Moab, Utah: Real People Press, 1989.

Andreas, Steve, and Connirae Andreas. *Change Your Mind—and Keep the Change.* Moab, Utah: Real People Press, 1987.

Bandler, Richard. *Magic in Action.* Cupertino, Calif.: Meta Publications, 1984.

Bandler, Richard. *Using Your Brain—For a Change.* Moab, Utah: Real People Press, 1985.

Bandler, Richard, and John Grinder. *Frogs into Princes.* Moab, Utah: Real People Press, 1979.

Bandler, Richard, and John Grinder. *Reframing: Neuro-Linguistic Programming and the Transformation of Meaning.* Moab, Utah: Real People Press, 1982.

Bandler, Richard, and John Grinder. *The Structure of Magic, Vol. 1.* Palo Alto, Calif.: Science and Behavior Books, 1975.

Bandler, Richard, and Will MacDonald. *An Insider's Guide to Sub-Modalities.* Cupertino, Calif.: Meta Publications, 1988.

Cameron-Bandler, Leslie. *They Lived Happily Ever After.* Cupertino, Calif.: Meta Publications, 1978.

Dilts, Robert. *Changing Belief Systems with NLP.* Cupertino, Calif.: Meta Publications, 1990.

Dilts, Robert B., et al. *Neuro-Linguistic Programming, Vol. 1.* Cupertino, Calif.: Meta Publications, 1980.

Grinder, John, and Richard Bandler. *The Structure of Magic, Vol. 2.* Palo Alto, Calif.: Science and Behavior Books, 1976.

Laborde, Genie Z. *Influencing with Integrity: Management Skills for Communication and Negotiation.* Palo Alto, Calif.: Science and Behavior Books, 1984.

Mackenzie, Marlin M., with Ken Denlinger. *Golf: The Mind Game.* New York: Dell Publishing, 1990.

McMaster, Michael, and John Grinder. *Precision: A New Approach to Communication.* Beverly Hills, Calif.: Precision Models, 1980.

Robbins, Anthony. *Unlimited Power.* New York: Simon and Schuster, 1986.

INDEX

Effort control, 31
Emotions:
   anchoring, *see* Anchoring
   beliefs and values affecting, 11
   blocking optimal performance,
      32–33
   emotional awareness exercise,
      171
   identifying K (kinesthetic) cues
      and, 21
   just-right, *see* Just-right emo-
      tional state
   metaskill techniques, *see*
      Metaskill techniques
   of the pros, 25
Energy, 31
Energy Anchor, 127
   evaluation of, 130
Energy regulation, 126–30
   Energy Anchor, 127, 130
   Energy Visualization, 127–30
   evaluation of, 130
Energy Visualization, 127–30
Enjoying yourself, 142, 145
Erickson, Betty, 114
   technique for self-hypnosis
      (modified), 114–15
Erickson, Dr. Milton H., 111, 135
Errors, unforced, *see* Unforced
   errors
Estep, Mike, 23–24, 93
Expectations about your tennis
   game, 141–42
External (uptime) cues, 23
   auditory, 159
   as contextual anchors, 23,
      38–39
   kinesthetic, 159–60
   of the pros:
      auditory, 25
      kinesthetic, 25–26
      visual, 24
   visual, 157–59

Fantasy match:
   Backup Process, 90–93

Competitive-State Anchor,
   63–65
Fatigue, 125, 126
   see also Energy regulation
Feedback, 8–9
Feedforward, 8–9
Focusing on what you do right, 3
Free-Swing Anchor, 86–87
Friendliness, 31
Fundamentals, 2–41
   Anchoring, 29–41
   Sherlock Holmes Exercise,
      15–27
   the warm-up, 3–13

Gallwey, Tim, 90
Game plans, 93–94
Get-It-Back Process, 104–105
Get-It Process, 98–104
   metaphorical anchor, 100–101,
      103–104
   steps in, 101–102
Getting Well Again (Simonton),
   135
Gibbs, Jon, 94
Graf, Steffi, 46–47
Gratz, Michael, 3–4, 13, 98–101,
   104–105
Grinder, John, 6
Gupta, "Tutu," 73

Hay fever, 137
Healing with metaskills techniques, 135–39
   ankle surgery, 136–37
   hay fever, 137
   knee surgery, 137
   steps in, 138
Hearing, *see* A (auditory) cues
Holographic Viewing, 105–106
Hope, 31
Hypnosis, *see* Self-hypnosis

Information processing, 7–10
Injuries, 125
Inner Tennis: Playing the Game
   (Gallwey), 90